PARTNERS

One Hundred Years of the
Calgary Police Service

By JACK PEACH

Based on research by
John Robertson

Published by Canadian Trade and Industry Publishing Group, Calgary, Alberta.

Printed in Canada.

Cover photo: With the Calgary skyline clearly visible in the background, members of the Calgary Police Service Mounted Patrol Unit pose with the flags of our country, our province, and our police service.

ACKNOWLEDGEMENTS

The Calgary Police Service wishes to thank the following people for their contributions to this book:

JOHN ROBERTSON, Past Curator, Calgary Police Service Museum/Archives, for the extensive research he undertook which forms the basis for this book;

ANNE CAPUNE, Administrator, Public Affairs Branch, for her diligence in editing the manuscript without changing Jack Peach's distinctive style; and for overseeing the tendering, production, and marketing of the book;

DAVID PARAMA, Curator, Calgary Police Service Museum/Archives, for conducting the final search and selection of photos; for writing the captions; for incorporating the photographic component with the written work; and for assisting with the editing, tendering, production, and marketing of the book;

SUPERINTENDENT NORM LUND, for his general guidance and assistance in editing and keeping the record straight on recent facts related to the operation of the Calgary Police Service;

The staff of the Calgary Police Service Identification Section, especially Barry Ogle, for much of the 1985 photographic work; and

The members of the Calgary Police Service, both serving and retired, who provided stories, photographs, and support for this project.

The police and the community are partners in maintaining the peace and security of Calgary. The community sets the standards. The police ensure those standards are maintained.

In 1883 the Canadian Pacific Railway reached Calgary. A significant event in the life of the fledgling community, everybody, including the NWMP, came out to witness the event.
(Photo: courtesy of the RCMP Museum, Regina)

When the railway reached Calgary on August 11, 1883 the end of the line was the east bank of the Elbow River. The first work train was greeted by the whole fledgling community of about 400 people. The entire pattern of their frontier life was about to change, for the railway's arrival marked a shift in the axis of trade and communication with "the outside world."

Ox teams had been the supply line along a south-north prairie trail used by many settlers arriving from Fort Benton on the Missouri River. They were about to make their final plodding trip for here was a new direct east-west link with the rest of Canada for people and commerce.

The community, made up of wooden-floored tents, some shanties, and a few wooden box-like business places, was vulnerable to every frontier peril. Even the security of Fort Calgary, manned by the North West Mounted Police, was on the west side of the unbridged Elbow. The guardianship of the knot of people was just another small burden added to the responsibilities of the garrison

Fort Calgary approximately 1882. In 1875 a fort, complete with palisade, was built at the confluence of the Bow and Elbow rivers. By 1882 the fort had been rebuilt, this time without a palisade.
(Photo: courtesy of the RCMP Museum, Regina)

of "redcoats" at the 8-year-old fort whose policing roles extended throughout a vast stretch of sparsely-occupied wilderness.

Fortunately for the mounties it was a peaceable time. The Indians were not troublesome, trappers and adventurers came and went through the community and, when there was a dust-up, a constable usually could be summoned to "show the flag."

The North West Mounted Police, by nature of their mandate and training, were the west's authority figure, and the fact they received their nationally-conceived policy directives from Ottawa tended to distance them from intimate community affairs.

Before the snow began to fly at the end of 1883 the railway-builders had moved west towards the mountainous spine of the continent. The Canadian Pacific Railway, with its eye on land values, set down its Calgary station west of the Elbow, not far from where it stands today. The settlement had to follow, to cluster near the station. The winter freeze-up made it possible to skid the more substantial buildings across the river ice. While the winter was still young trainloads of newcomers were arriving, and the infant town began to inherit the moral ills of those who chose to live shoulder-to-shoulder in the struggle to establish themselves and their community.

There was an urgent need for the selection, from their own number, of leaders capable of organizing a pattern of authority in matters of administration and orderly harmony. The townsfolk and the mounted police at least were on the same side of the Elbow, but nobody wanted to have them maintain law and order even though rowdyism and quarrels were increasing as the town sprouted at a very brisk pace.

By February 1884 there already had been a murder committed during a robbery and the culprit caught and swiftly sentenced, and hanged at the fort. Settlers who ran afoul of the law were fined, the money being remitted to Ottawa by the federal lawmen. Obviously this was seen as interference in community affairs as well

This advertisement appeared in The Calgary Herald on January 16, 1884. With the townsite finally located on the west side of the Elbow River, however, lots to the east of the Elbow were seen as less desirable.
(Ad: courtesy of the Glenbow Archives)

as a loss in the form of local capital and revenue. So, when a town meeting was called with a view to incorporating Calgary as a town in charge of its own affairs, response was enthusiastic.

Of the approximately 500 residents, 428 signatures were affixed to a petition, the required fee was collected and, on November 17, 1884 Calgary received federal permission to become the first community in the Northwest Territories to become a town.

Almost immediately there followed an enthusiastic election with no fewer than 10 per cent of the people proclaiming themselves as candidates! When the ballots were counted saddlemaker George Murdoch was our first mayor with councilmen S.J.Hogg, Dr.Neville Lindsay, J.H.Millward, and S.J.Clarke.

Calgary's first town council. Left to right (standing): Councillor S.J. Hogg; Assessor J. Campbell; Solicitor H. Bleeker; Councillors Dr. N.J. Lindsay; J.H. Millward, and S.J.Clarke; Police Chief J.S. Ingram; Collector J.S. Douglas; and Councillor I.S. Freeze. Seated: Mayor George Murdoch; Treasurer C. Sparrow; Clerk T.T.A. Boys.
(Photo: courtesy of the Glenbow Archives)

One of the five standing committees named at that first council meeting of December 4, 1884 was given the job of writing some bylaws including one dealing with the selection of a police officer of determination and authority.

From the four job applications the mayor and council chose former Winnipeg chief constable Jack S.Ingram who became Calgary's first policeman. He had a fair record as a Manitoba sheriff in 1873 and as Winnipeg's first chief of police in 1874. What really won him the Calgary job was his performance and reputation as a down-to-earth hotel-keeper who, in 1883 with a partner, had opened the Central Hotel on Atlantic Avenue .

Councillors soft-pedalled a shadow on Ingram's mid-west past for alleged over-friendliness with a certain prairie bawdy house. Perhaps they were not to be as sure of the wisdom of their decision once the strongly Methodist-minded Calgary Herald boomed editorially in March 1884:

"It is to be lamented that the voice of prostitution is sullying so deeply the first page of Calgary's history....The people of Calgary are asking themselves the question if the police are going to allow this promising town to become the asylum for the harlots and prostitutes of the east."

Jack S. Ingram, Calgary's first chief of police, held the position from February 1885 to March 13, 1888. *(Photo: Calgary Police Service Archives)*

The paper, of course, had been addressing the question to the only force at the time, the North West Mounted Police.

Calgary's own town police force was still a few months away from its date of creation, February 7, 1885, when Chief Jack Ingram assumed duties that had been assigned Constable Jack Campbell up to that point. He was a good man for the job. He could handle tense situations, he had the experience, physical attributes, and demeanour to see that his orders were obeyed. If Jack Ingram had a fault it was his independence for he resented interference. However the councillor he worked with most closely was Simon J. Clarke, an ex-mountie with an equally tough manner, and the two got along very well.

Unfortunately the appointment of Ingram was no cure-all, for the local situation remained rather prickly. On one hand there was the federal force, so self-contained it investigated crimes, arrested suspects, judged and prosecuted them, and maintained the jail in which convicted persons were held.

On the other hand Chief Ingram investigated local infractions, arrested suspects, and brought them before Mayor Murdoch who presided over the town's court in his capacity as Chief Magistrate and Justice of the Peace. Unhappily, at that point in his law-enforcement pursuits, Ingram had to ask North West Mounted Police fort commander Colonel Herchmer if he could please use a cell or two until a municipal lock-up was built. Herchmer not only refused, he had his constables arrest another local vagrant right under Ingram's nose!

Looking east along Stephen Avenue, Calgary's major thoroughfare in 1885. This wide avenue was a favorite place to break horses, much to the chagrin of Chief Constable Ingram.
(Photo: courtesy of the Glenbow Archives)

Colonel Herchmer was in a snit anyway, unhappy about the new town next to his fort. Back on the night of November 17, about 2 months before Calgary's new policeman took office, he had been set upon by some town toughs and tossed off the Elbow River bridge. The men, who obviously had a lethal grudge against the commanding officer of Fort Calgary, were never apprehended, and Herchmer prudently steered clear of the townspeople's hostility.

Mayor Murdoch was not impressed by Herchmer's pique, for one of the main reasons for incorporation was to give the town power to enforce its bylaws and to keep the fines that, when levied by the mounties, had been remitted in their entirety to Ottawa.

When the mounted police, rather than his own lawmen, arrested a vagrant in town the mayor's fiery public criticism of the federal force was reported with alacrity by the newspaper. This was the core of his annoyance: **"We are a body corporate with full powers granted us to regulate and govern our own sanitary and moral affairs. We do not want and will not tolerate outsiders' interference with them....**

"We have an officer under order and pay especially to attend to such matters and the ordinance gives us full power to deal with

them within our limits but these gentlemen not knowing how to act in a courteous spirit towards this Council, it becomes the duty of the board to take such steps as will place it beyond their power to interfere with us in any manner whatever."

With authorities of the town of Calgary and of the mounted police obviously on a collision course, the hand of the Lord stayed the exchange of any bruises by making it mandatory for most of the federal police to mount up and gallop off to confront warring factions of the Riel Rebellion whose tempers were flaring to alarming proportions. In the redcoats' absence Chief Ingram consolidated his position in the town but, unfortunately, for only a short time. Upon their return to Calgary the mounties picked up where they had left off, especially in the area of enforcing the town's liquor laws.

Their interference was abetted by the arrival, in September 1885, of a new stipendiary magistrate, Jeremiah Travis, an implacable teetotaller obsessed with the idea that a liquor ring was running Calgary. Travis never did become a westerner except to feather his nest with Calgary real estate before his recall by Ottawa.

While he was here Travis was a large burr under Calgary's saddle-blanket. For example he had plain-clothes mounties without a search warrant raid Councillor Clarke's saloon. That caper resulted in Clarke's arrest and a 6-month sentence which created a town uproar. A later spectacular tangle between Travis and the editor of the Herald newspaper found rebellious Chief Ingram riding in a cheerful, noisy parade that escorted the editor to the mounted-police lockup!

Town morale was further eroded by Travis' interference in the civic election of 1886. He charged that council had tampered with the voters' list, and appointed a mayor and quartet of councillors of his own choosing. Calgary found itself with dual governing bodies, one elected, one appointed, both in disagreement! In the ensuing turmoil the town's toughs took full advantage of the political stalemate. Word quickly spread that Calgary offered easy pickings and, because of the administrative in-fighting, little danger of police interference. In fact Chief Ingram, after working without pay for three months, decided to abandon the job.

With no town police force Calgary experienced its first crime wave. Four miles from town a man was murdered in broad daylight, the Calgary-Edmonton stage coach was robbed at gunpoint, and a number of ranch houses suffered break-and-entry forays. No rewards were collected and nobody was apprehended for these crimes. Finally, in October 1886, the North West Territories Council declared all 1886 Calgary elections void and called for a new one.

With ex-mountie, now postmaster, George King as mayor and four newly-elected councillors the business of running Calgary soon was brought under control. Not only did the new administration re-appoint Jack Ingram police chief, it appointed three town constables, at last providing the chief with some help to reinstate a proper degree of law and order in the community.

The four-man team was too successful for, toward the end of 1886, council decided the large force was an extravagance and laid off one constable. A.E.Shelton, a council member, noting the drop in local crime, had been campaigning vigorously to further reduce the force. As soon as he was elected mayor in 1888 Shelton fired another officer, leaving only Chief Jack Ingram and Constable Robert Barker to keep Calgarians in line.

Irking the chief even more Shelton decided to take over the daily running of the service in the belief that he knew more about policing than did Ingram. He achieved that simply by naming himself Chief of the Police and Relief Committee. To drive home the point Shelton raided a gambling game and, for his pains, received Ingram's resignation.

From eight applicants for the police chief's job Shelton chose an ex-Ottawa policeman who operated a lumber business in Calgary, Matthew Sylvester Dillabough. To Shelton's credit he made it very clear that the new man was chief in name only, that the top cop was Chairman of the Police and Relief Committee, namely himself. Then he instructed Dillabough and his assisting constable that gamblers and prostitutes were to be left alone. They were. In all of 1888 not a single raid was recorded.

Matthew S. Dillabough, shown here with his children, was chief of police from March 1888 to April 1890.
(Photo: Calgary Police Service Archives)

Shelton's hands-off policy resulted in the establishment of a pretty seamy side to Calgary's otherwise fresh-faced pioneer atmosphere from which, with considerable success, visitors and potential customers of real estate promoters were shielded. Even the Herald newspaper looked benignly upon a newly-opened billiard emporium as evidence of the innocent boomtown spirit of the community. Known as the Turf Club it was never raided by the police, not even after D.W.Marsh was elected to the mayor's chair in place of Shelton. Only when a young Indian was murdered there by one of the town's popular roughnecks, William "Jumbo" Fisk, did the law step in. After a sordid, convoluted pair of trials, Fisk was convicted but Calgary's reputation was sullied. The whole town agreed it was high time the police cleaned up their act and got things back on track.

That was more easily said than done for Fisk's cohorts still cluttered the scene. Chief Dillabough lacked the toughness the situation called for, something the town's other policeman, Constable Barker, resented. But then an election in 1890 produced more clumsy political interference.

Calgary, as seen from the North Hill in 1890. The street running south, just left of the center of the photograph, is 1 Street East.
(Photo: courtesy of the Glenbow Archives)

Dr.James Lafferty became Calgary's fifth mayor, bringing to the office some very autocratic attitudes. He saw to it that Dillabough was reduced to the rank of constable so that the two lawmen could carry out their duties on an equal footing under the terms of a new document of Orders and Regulations. This alternate policing policy required constables Dillabough and Barker each to work a 12-hour day, 7 days a week, one on night shift, the other on day shift, which they were to swap every two weeks.

The two policemen constantly were at loggerheads. They worked independently, not discussing their activities, yet harboring a common resentment over the mayoralty interference. Dr.Lafferty announced his intention of seeking re-election and of reducing the police force to one volunteer uniformed man on day-shift, and just a watchman at night. Fortunately James Reilly won the election and endorsed his electioneering intention of upgrading the police force by firing the two constables and advertising for new men.

An ex-Winnipeg police sergeant, Thomas English, was chosen for the chief's post. To complete the clean sweep, although Dillabough and Barker were among the applicants, the mayor and council selected James Fraser and Albert Ross as constables. By the summer of 1891 Ross, not having lived up to expectations, was released. Chief English was a no-nonsense policeman and, with Constable Fraser, quickly cleaned up the town.

The mayor was still Chairman of the Police and Relief Committee and councillors were far too keen to interfere in police business, making the chief's role anything but an easy one. The next annual civic election, in 1892, put former councillor Alexander Lucas in the mayor's chair.

Thomas English, whose frontier style of law enforcement sometimes landed him in trouble, was chief from 1891 to 1909.
(Photo: Calgary Police Service Archives)

Suddenly a diversion gripped the little town when, in June 1892, a newly-arrived Chinese brought smallpox with him from the west coast. His fellow countrymen hid him for a few days, but as soon as word got out, Chief English, acting on orders from council, quarantined the sick man in a shack a short distance beyond the outskirts of town. Its location, of course, brought the mounted police into the matter with everyone grossly over-reacting.

A local carpenter came down with smallpox and he too was banished to the quarantine camp under mounted police guard. A squabble between the mounties and town police over the sick man's possessions ended with a furious Chief English, in handcuffs, being confined to the mounted police barracks.

The mayor bailed him out and the case against him for having assaulted a mountie had to be postponed because the witnesses were ill! Actually the charges were dropped, and the mayor felt it prudent that Thomas English take a nerve-soothing holiday back in his old stomping ground — Winnipeg. To fill the gap during the chief's absence a new constable, Thomas Leppington, was hired to keep peace in town.

Unfortunately other local Chinese had contracted smallpox from the newcomer they had sheltered, so they too had to be isolated in the camp under the scrutiny of the mounted police. On the night of August 2, having been examined and declared free of smallpox, the patients were released. Because, obviously, they were headed back into town away from their jurisdiction the mounties washed their hands of the whole affair. However, they didn't know that in town the matter of Chinese being admitted to Calgary in the first place had boiled over as a racist issue. A mob was waiting for the unfortunate men to cross the town limits.

Angry Calgarians had been torching and vandalizing Chinese property, the police chief was in Winnipeg, Constable Leppington was a greenhorn, and the mayor insisted the Chinese now were the mounties' responsibility. So, here were these convalescents, returning to town in the gathering darkness to be confronted with anger and destruction and no sign of protection. The mayor, just before leaving town for the evening allegedly to visit friends, had given Constable Fraser the night off and ordered rookie Constable Leppington to patrol as usual.

Immediately the mounties, upon hearing that mobs were on the prowl trashing Chinese property in defiance of Leppington, rushed into town. They broke up the mobs and took ten Chinese into protective custody. Even Mayor Lucas realized his mistake and scurried back into town to wire Tom English in Winnipeg to hurry home. The mounties continued to patrol the town that was still in a smoldering mood, until Chief English returned by train to take charge of the situation.

The aftermath of all that was a sea of turbulent rhetoric with everyone passing the buck and dodging the responsibility. Constable Leppington was known to have witnessed the whole ugly affair. Being alone and inexperienced, he had wisely chosen to remain in the background, firmly believing his visibility would just have served to inflame the mob.

After a lot of civic gum-gnashing the Chinese were fully compensated. Alderman Cushing, an outspoken critic of the police and the civic administrators, was disgusted by the whole mess. He recommended that the municipal police be disbanded and the mounties given the task of policing Calgary. Providentially his angry proposal fell on deaf ears.

Chief English got on with his job, Leppington's position on the force was confirmed, and shortly thereafter another mayor took the helm. This new chief magistrate was Wesley Orr, a forthright man of action, and the first elected mayor of the now City of Calgary; the community had achieved that status on the day he took office. He shrewdly refused the position of Chairman of the Police and Relief Committee, the first mayor to do so. By this simple, sensible, and very crucial decision, he set a pattern.

In 1892 Calgary's police force posed with some of the leading citizens of the day. Standing (left to right) are: Paddy Nolan, K.C.; Chief T. English; Cst. Fraser; Cst. Leppington; Senator James Lougheed. Seated (left to right) are: Alderman Wesley Orr; Unknown; City Solicitor A.L. Sifton.
(Photo: courtesy of the Glenbow Archives)

From then on, the committee's chairman was selected from the aldermanic ranks and the mayor no longer was in the position to play the role of police chief. At last the men of the force were freed to keep peace in the community without being bedeviled by politics or any further talk of being replaced by mounted police.

Calgary entered the twentieth century with a population of 4,000 and a police force of two, the chief and his constable. Within ten years 40,000 people called Calgary their home and were under the protection of 36 "plain-clothes" and "uniforms." But one outstanding man did not survive the decade. Big Tom English, the almost legendary, walrus-mustachioed police chief, was regarded by too many city administrators as more of a relic of frontier days than a leader of modern law enforcers.

The man's simple honesty and lack of guile became his liabilities. City commissioners leaped on an undistinguished event to pry the old chief loose from the job he had held for 19 years. English had a staunch ally in The Calgary Herald but The Morning Albertan was out to get him. That paper pounced on the chief's handling of a petty gambling offence that recently had taken place at the Calgary Stampede, and it publicly worried the matter to death. The man-in-the-street was on the chief's side but to

This 1904 photo shows Chief English and his men, along with others, outside the multipurpose police office, city hall, and jail at 702 Drinkwater Street.
(Photo: courtesy of the Glenbow Archives)

Calgary's police force in 1908.
(Photo: Calgary Police Service Archives)

no avail, for Tom English was given his walking papers in July 1909 at the age of 62 in those days of no pension plans or unemployment insurance. The popular veteran of many stormy confrontations with city officials and a regime he and the citizens were proud to record as being free of serious crime was replaced by his deputy, Thomas Mackie.

As a result of Mackie's 1910 report that centred upon a plea for a larger, mobile force, a 10-place patrol van was quickly provided. The paddy wagon soon became widely known as the "Black Maria," a great improvement over the department's horse and democrat.

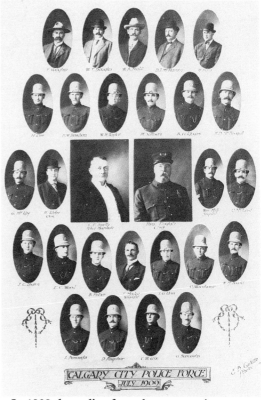

In 1909 the police force began wearing 'Boston-style' helmets. This was also the year that Chief English was fired.
(Photo: Calgary Police Service Archives)

A car for the chief's use came along 6 years later! The area of the city had grown substantially, street cars were serving newly-established residential and industrial areas on all sides of the downtown core, and there was an increasing need for policing flexibility and mobility.

Thomas Mackie replaced Thomas English as chief in 1909. With this promotion, Mackie became the first man to have worked his way up to chief from the rank of constable.
(Photo: Calgary Police Service Archives)

Operating within the confines of his limited budget Chief Mackie added a four-horse-and-rider mounted section to the roster in 1911 and a year later helped the force take a giant step by establishing four branch sub-stations. Next he was able to create a separate detective squad headed by Detective Sergeant W.A.Nutt, and the department's men began feeling at last they really were out there among the people in all parts of the little city.

The mounted branch varied in number from the days it was first tried out in the summer of 1910 and felt to be well worth considering as a permanent addition. With residential areas well established on both sides of the Bow and the Elbow rivers, there was a need for communication that was a bit faster and more direct than a constable reaching an outlying scene by street car or on foot. Weather permitting, a mounted constable could effectively reach a trouble-spot in a short time and, on his horse, exert a calming and subduing influence. This was particularly true since the mounted policemen's accomplished western riding skill was matched by the stern regimental bearing of rider and horse.

The first 'Black Maria' owned by the Calgary police was purchased in 1911. Manufactured by the White Company of Cleveland, it was powered by a 38-horsepower, four-cylinder engine and had a top speed of 45 mph. *(Photo: Calgary Police Service Archives)*

Driver Robert Cunliff and Inspector W. A. Nutt in an automobile purchased primarily for the use of the chief in 1916. *(Photo: Calgary Police Service Archives)*

Heading the riders was Sergeant Ralph S. Kendall, a veteran of "E" Division of the R.N.W.M.P. and of the South African war. Although

English-born, Kendall had become a complete western Canadian, even spending his spare time writing stirring tales of the old west and its red-coat police. A couple of his books, "Benton of the Mounted" and "The Luck of the Mounted" were a great success when marketed in Canada, the United States, and the British Isles.

By 1912 many Calgary streets had come a long way from the mud roads of the 1890s. *(Photo: courtesy of the Provincial Archives of Alberta)*

In 1910 the City Mounted Police wore high helmets and rode rented horses. *(Photo: courtesy of Glenbow Archives)*

City Mounted Police approximately 1913. The high Boston helmets had been given up in favor of the flat forage cap during Chief Mackie's tenure. With Chief Cuddy, however, bobby-style helmets (shown here) soon appeared as part of the uniform.
(Photo: courtesy of Provincial Archives of Alberta)

Kendall and his mounted squad were impressive working performers at large Calgary holiday gatherings including street parades, regular assignments on crowd and vehicular traffic control, parking, and at stray animal round-ups that in those early days constituted a frequent problem.

One of Chief Mackie's great burdens was the extent of the city's gambling and prostitution and the resultant violence.

The sin centre that attracted the community's black sheep was pinpointed as a cafeteria on 8th Avenue run by Burt and Johnnie Reid. The Reid brothers for two frustrating years had been laughing at the unsuccessful efforts of the force to catch them breaking the law. Finally Mackie put together a caper that can be chalked up as the first big raid in Calgary.

The attack was planned in small, isolated segments to preserve the element of surprise. Then, one Saturday night all the pieces were brought together. For example, Chief Mackie reached the front doorstep of his home in the usual way whereupon, by design, he was swept up by a patrol headed for the cafeteria.

The outwitted Reid brothers were livid. The upper and main floors were crowded with patrons, many of them illegally drinking. Three young women barricaded a door despite commands from the chief to let him enter. When the women relented they were all alone, claiming to be chambermaids and roomers.

Things got a bit tacky when it was reported that the mayor and two city commissioners had been spotted among the surprised "guests." Chief Thomas Mackie was too much of a gentleman to pursue the matter, even privately. However, rumors persisted, including one that claimed his discovery of the indiscretion was the reason Chief Mackie resigned his position later that year.

Burt Reid abandoned that line of work following the raid but his brother Johnnie moved his operation to South Coulee, not far from today's Chinook Centre, transforming the hitherto quiet Manchester working-man's suburb into a wide-open red-light district.

Those years closely preceding the Great War were difficult for the police. A real estate boom filled the community with new residents, land speculators, and all manner of get-rich-quick artists. On November 11, 1911 the battered body of John Middleton was found in an empty lot on 9th Avenue, and a former mounted police sergeant, given the rank of detective by Mayor Mitchell, was assigned to the case. Detective Tucker not only is unfavorably remembered as being responsible for Calgary having its first unsolved murder, but also for viciously turning on his chief, making him the scapegoat for his own incompetence.

When Chief Mackie resigned on the heels of Tucker's dismissal The Calgary Herald launched a campaign calling for an outsider to

Chief Mackie with the 1911 Calgary City Police Force.
(Photo: Calgary Police Service Archives)

head the force. The newspaper gave high marks to Tom English's regime and deplored the political interference that became his downfall. Now it was Mackie's turn after 9 years' service. Editorially, on June 16, 1919, the Herald trumpeted the call for a new chief with enough strength and distancing to resist political pressure.

"What Calgary wants is a strong man...who shall be an autocrat within the four walls of his office. Of all the branches of civic administration, no position requires less interference than that of a chief of police force. His judgments should be final beyond which there should be no appeal. If these judgments should prove to be wrong he can be removed, but he should have an unhampered opportunity to effect his department's reforms and to bring it to a state of efficiency without outside dictation."

Inspector W.A.Nutt was appointed Acting Chief, a popular choice, but the Herald belligerently opposed Nutt or any other internal candidate for the permanent job. Moreover, said the paper, the chief's salary should be raised from its current $1,500 a year to $3,500. When word got out that this campaigning might be successful, applicants for the chief's job poured in. The deputy chief of Toronto's force offered his services for $5,000; the city countered with $4,500, but he refused.

From a list of 65 applicants city council chose Alfred Cuddy with 30 years on the Toronto force and a reputation of being firm and fair, a street-wise no-nonsense policeman. Chief Cuddy, who arrived in Cal-

gary in the spring of 1912, wasted no time implementing some far-reaching changes. Obviously he enjoyed the city fathers' confidence for he tackled sizeable manpower, equipment, and facilities problems promptly and vigorously.

Having declared at the outset that he had under him "a splendid force," Cuddy found the premises on the ground floor of City Hall to be inadequate from the standpoint of working space and the requirement of confidentiality. He quickly persuaded council to allocate monies for the construction of a new, separate, police headquarters equipped with the latest law-enforcement aids.

Inspector W.A. Nutt was appointed acting chief in 1912 after T. Mackie resigned. *(Photo: Calgary Police Service Archives)*

The brick and sandstone building east of City Hall at 333 7th Avenue East was opened in the summer of 1914. In it was a central communication system connected with 67 new curb-side call boxes spotted throughout the city, and with four substations, each manned by sergeants and constables who were knowledgeable residents of those particular areas.

The old City Hall and police office building, erected in 1885, stands dwarfed by the new sandstone building still under construction in 1910. In 1911 the police occupied offices on the ground floor of the new building.
(Photo: Calgary Police Service Archives)

Alfred Cuddy came from Toronto to take over as chief of police in the spring of 1912.
(Photo: Calgary Police Service Archives)

Police charge office in the new City Hall, 1912.
(Photo: Calgary Police Service Archives)

This photograph, taken sometime after 1918, shows City Hall with the police headquarters building behind it. Chief Alfred Cuddy successfully argued for the new facility, which was opened in 1914.
(Photo: Calgary Police Service Archives)

Police headquarters at 333 - 7 Avenue S.E. as it appeared in 1922.
(Photo: Calgary Police Service Archives)

Signal room in the new police headquarters building. The constable is sitting at a switchboard capable of handling up to eight calls at a time! Behind him is the call box system equipment, which provided police at headquarters and field personnel with a fast, reliable means of communication.
(Photo: Calgary Police Service Archives)

This map showing call box and substation locations in Calgary was part of a signal system installation report written by police electrician J.M. Rudolph in August 1915. *(Photo: Calgary Police Service Archives)*

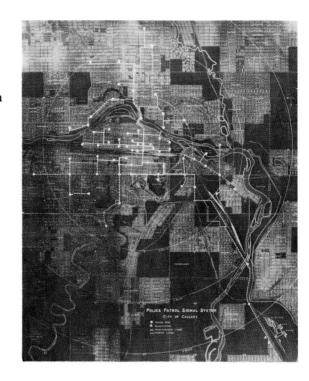

Early photo of a call box standard. Note the light for night calls and the bells for day calls. *(Photo: Calgary Police Service Archives)*

This 1950 photograph shows a call box standard with both police call box equipment and a fire alarm pull station. *(Photo: courtesy of the Provincial Archives of Alberta)*

Number 2 police and fire station still stands at 1801 - 2 Street S.E. This photo
was taken approximately 1920.
(Photo: courtesy of the Glenbow Archives)

Police and fire station located on the corner of 17 Avenue and 20 Street W.,
1922. Police occupied the left-hand portion of the building.
(Photo: Calgary Police Service Archives)

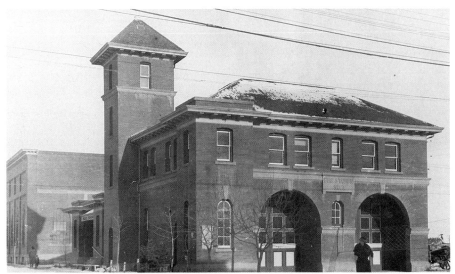

Police and fire station located at 140 - 10 Avenue N.W. The portion of the building which appears behind the tower in this photo was occupied by city police.
(Photo: Calgary Police Service Archives)

Chief Cuddy appointed Detective Joe Carruthers as head of a new Identification Bureau with the latest Century camera. He required every convicted prisoner to be photographed and fingerprinted. He ordered a new Indian motorcycle for use in traffic control but, after it proved unreliable, the 1912 machine was disposed of in favour of the addition of two riders and horses to the mounted unit.

It was a period of building for Chief Cuddy who set himself the goal of converting the force from a small town, to a professional city police department. Even though Calgary police still had one unsolved 1911 murder on the books and in 1912 were confronted with six killings, two of which remained a puzzle, it was publicly felt that the force was doing its best during difficult times.

Of course Chief Cuddy was a shrewd operator for, in 1914, he made a point of obtaining a pay raise for everyone and formalizing working conditions for all, from the elevator operator, dog catcher, matron, and signal man, to the chief of police. The public was informed of this and

The Calgary City Police Detective Department is shown here on the steps of City Hall in 1912. The boy (front row center) is Jack Cuddy.
(Photo: Calgary Police Service Archives)

could see the chief's influence on the streets when once again constables wore helmets, as they had in English's time, and were proud to be identified as Third, Second, or First Grade.

The firmness of the chief's leadership was evident around town. Instead of being a reactive force, the police went forth to stage continual raids on gambling and bawdy houses. Operators of questionable businesses were invited to the chief's office and told to close shop or move out of town. If they were merely to change addresses within the city, they could expect a constant stream of raids, fines, and jail terms. By 1913 South Coulee had returned to quiet residential respectability.

For all the drastic changes there were lumpy matters in the chief's life, especially after he had jockeyed himself and his men into a position of being looked to, by the public, for guidance and leadership. It happened that a new dance craze called the tango was sweeping the nation. Calgarians, curious to learn the dance, were reminded that apparently the Bishop of Paris had declared the dance to be sinful. Of course that made it all the more intriguing, although Cuddy pontificated that "I think the introduction of the tango would be a bad thing for Calgary."

However, after having been granted a showing of the dance in company with Alderman T.A.P. "Tappy" Frost, Chief Cuddy did not even rate mention in the press with his opinion, so the tango and the chief — stayed. Unfortunately, many of the police force did not. There were 91 policemen and 9 civilians on strength, of whom 13 had come from Ireland, 30 from England, 32 from Scotland, and the Canadian-born members of the force numbered 22.

Small wonder, with the Mother Country calling for help in the Great War, the chief had no choice but to release them by letting go a few at a time in order to preserve as much police coverage as possible. Despite that, by 1916 the manpower of the force was less than half the 1914 figure. The shortage forced the closure of the valuable sub-stations and the reduction of the mounted force from six to four. Those uniformed men who remained had their work cut out for them on most strenuous terms.

Sarcee Camp, established on Elbow River benchland southwest of the city, at its peak had 15,000 soldiers-in-training under canvas. Young and vigorous, these men spoiled for the good time that was available to them during off-duty hours in town. A streetcar line served the camp but the last run was at 10 o'clock at night. Soldiers, stranded in town, risked law-

Troops leaving Calgary for the east and then Europe. Many city police members would follow these men over the course of the war.
(Photo: courtesy of the Glenbow Archives)

These Calgary police officers were among those who answered the call to arms during World War I. Of them, Detective David Milne, Constable A. Moire, Constable P. Nicholson, and Constable G. Wilson gave their lives. *(Photo: Calgary Police Service Archives)*

breaking rather than military punishment for returning late to camp. So car theft, without malice, was the soldiers' favorite solution to the problem. Nine times out of ten the stolen car, undamaged, would be found by the police outside the camp's main gate.

More serious were the problems created by civilians and soldiers from the proliferation of gambling, prostitution, drunkenness, and brawling. Then the hitherto high-spirited behaviour of the young men in khaki turned ugly on the night of February 16, 1916. A rumour reached camp that a returned soldier, on staff at the White Lunch restaurant on 8th Avenue, had been replaced by a man of Austrian descent. The proprietor, Frank Nagel, proved the rumour to be false, but only after the damage had been done.

Chief Cuddy and about 15 constables, all he could muster at the time, confronted 500 soldiers spoiling for a showdown. The police were armed but the chief had made it clear guns were to be used only for personal protection. Soon it was obvious that talk was to no avail for, suddenly, a rock shattered the restaurant's plate-glass window. Pushing aside the police, the soldiers surged into the White Lunch and completely trashed it.

While this was going on, another mob of soldiers attacked the second White Lunch a couple of blocks away, destroying everything within it in a matter of minutes. The mob on 8th Avenue, by now well beyond reason and control, boiled upstairs and demolished the McLellan Dance Academy, owned by an innocuous Scot. Into town from Sarcee Camp rushed General George Cruikshank who managed to calm the rioters and persuade them, although they were still angry, to return to their barracks.

However, on the following night off-duty soldiers staged a frightening encore. It took them only 20 minutes to wreck the Riverside Hotel, located at the north end of Langevin Bridge, an attack based on hearsay that the proprietor had a German name.

Another group of soldiers, fired up by liquor and the excitement, headed for two 8th Avenue restaurants they were determined to demolish. This time the entire police force stood ready with drawn batons.

In 1916 the Riverside Hotel was destroyed by a mob of over-zealous off-duty soldiers who thought the owner had a German name.
(Photo: courtesy of the Glenbow Archives)

The weather, rather than the heat of battle, broke up the fray. It was too chilly for the soldiers to tackle such odds, so the groups broke up and returned to camp. For weeks afterwards special patrols were on duty throughout the downtown business district, successfully preventing any further trouble. Obviously, measured by these hair-raising events, a handful of police could not avert such vicious destruction of property by a mob fired up with liquor. The upshot was that throughout Alberta, effective July 1, 1916, it became illegal to possess or consume alcohol in public, which included liquor drinking in restaurants and automobiles. That new law created a troublesome but satisfying policing job for Chief Cuddy and his men.

The new legislation whittled the vending of liquor to two outlets, one in Calgary and one in Edmonton. The Calgary dispenser was the Rev. John McDougall, an obvious choice to ensure alcohol purchases were for medicinal purposes only! Sidestepping the law always has been a favorite indoor and outdoor sport and Calgarians back then were on the first-string team.

Liquor could be ordered from British Columbia, so every train arriving from the west was met by a large crowd clamoring for fast, personal service from the C.P.Express staff. Such large crowds appeared at train time that police had to be dispatched to direct traffic at the 9th Avenue and Centre Street depot.

The police enforced the new liquor regulations with enthusiasm until it was learned that the substantial revenue from fines was fattening provincial, rather than civic, coffers. Consequently the fervour of enforcement dwindled somewhat. Except, that is, in the case of Detective Tom Turner, an ex-Toronto policeman who had followed Chief Cuddy to the west. Turner, an exceptionally enthusiastic nemesis of liquor law violators, even set a record for Calgary's quickest arrest and prosecution.

In September 1916 the detective came across a man with a bottle in public, arrested him, brought him before the magistrate where he was convicted. The culprit paid the fine of $50 and was back out on the street. The whole affair took only 15 minutes!

Tom Turner interrupted some soldiers drinking in a public place and arrested them. Four of the men were recruits, and the fifth had just returned from action in Europe. Turner had the five quickly processed and, because they did not have the price of a fine, the magistrate sentenced each of them to 30 days in jail. When the news reached Sarcee Camp another riot was born.

This time a stone-throwing mob descended upon police headquarters, yelling for Tom Turner to show himself. Instead, above their noise, Chief Cuddy explained the law-breakers were not in that building. Moreover, he allowed a small delegation of them to inspect the cells, all of which were empty. The soldiers huddled, then decided that if their buddies were not in city cells, they must be in the hands of the mounties based at the old court house.

While a crowd of 1,000 curious onlookers milled outside, the soldiers made a shambles of the interior, chucking furniture out the windows where it was piled and set alight by some of the thrill seekers on the street. Then there was gunfire, a soldier was wounded, and the rioters and mounties really began fighting. While the fray escalated, some army lads set off to break into hardware stores to obtain arms and ammunition.

They were met by Inspector Nutt and a flying squad of city police who were still holding them at bay when army officers arrived from the camp. The promise of an investigation into the whole matter convinced the soldiers to disperse, thus defusing an explosive situation.

Most observers seemed to feel the principal fault lay with the over-zealous police. Obviously it was essential for the force to be a part of the community, working with it and for it; and that the Tom Turner type of policeman, dogmatically upholding the law, could have no place on the team. Not surprisingly, Turner was dismissed in 1919 for **"behaviour unbecoming a Calgary constable."**

For Calgary's police force those Great War years of 1914-1918 were a solemn challenge. With so many of their colleagues overseas and with thousands of transient troops in and around the city, lawmen of the force were thinly spread. Evidence of this struck home on the night of July 1/2, 1917. Constable Arthur "Sandy" Duncan failed to call in at 1:00 a.m. from his position on the beat. The duty sergeant was puzzled, but only when Duncan was not heard from at 2:00 in the morning, did he feel he could be spared to go out in search of the constable. Not finding a trace of Duncan he returned to wait it out.

At 5:00 a.m. a laborer on his way to work phoned headquarters to report an injured policeman in a downtown lane. It was Duncan, murdered they determined later, just after midnight on his beat by burglars he surprised at their cache at 8th Avenue and 8th Street West. Duncan was the first Calgary policeman to be killed on duty and, despite a provincial and city reward totalling $1,000, whoever killed him was never brought to justice.

The European battlefields continued to exact their toll of Calgary policemen, and by the beginning of 1919 Chief Alfred Cuddy's

This newspaper article on the murder of Constable Duncan appeared in The Calgary Herald on July 3, 1917.
(Photo: The Calgary Herald)

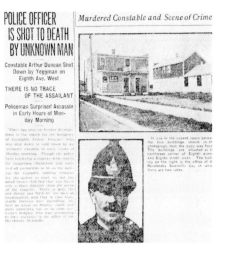

Constable Arthur Duncan's funeral procession.
(Photo: Calgary Police Service Archives)

work strength was reduced to 51, including the civilians, such as office help and tradesmen, attached to the force. But he used his manpower skillfully, leaving the reduced force well-regarded by the community when he resigned at the end of July 1919, to help create the new Alberta Provincial Police in the role of its commissioner.

Throughout the years between its formation and the departure of head man Chief Alfred Cuddy in 1919, the Calgary police force had been a man's world. Even the drain on personnel created by World War I did nothing to spur the appointment of women to the ranks. Even when city council, in the spring of 1914, created the position for a lady detective at a salary of $75 a month, Chief Cuddy grumpily declared that if a woman was taken on strength he would not give that person anything to do and, in fact, would tender his resignation. **He said, "I am firmly of the opinion that the woman who would be suitable for the position has yet to be born...!"**

Prior to World War II the only woman hired by the police was the matron whose job it was to look after the female prisoners. Usually the matron was the caretaker's wife, paid a few dollars for being on call when needed, day or night. Her duties included searching "...all female prisoners arrested for theft or other offences, as occasion may require." Also "she has charge of and cares for all female prisoners confined either as prisoners or witnesses, runaways, etc., and renders such assistance to them as may appear necessary."

In those days police work was considered a domain of men only. Even the secretaries and clerks were male and it was not until the mid-1940s that the attitude changed.

With the resignation of Alfred Cuddy in 1919, instead of reaching out for a new chief of police, Calgary City Council let it be known that although all applications were welcome, the appointment likely would come from within the force.

The three most likely candidates were Inspector D.Richardson, Inspector W.A.Nutt, and Detective D.Ritchie. Out of 32 applicants, David Ritchie was chosen even though he was a junior candidate. However he had been on the force since 1911 and had been awarded the Military Cross for gallantry in the Canadian Army overseas.

Chief Ritchie took over the top police post on September 15, 1919, beginning what was to become a memorable 22-year leadership. As with his predecessors, Ritchie immediately tackled matters he felt required changing, foremost of which was departmental behaviour, to which he introduced a military stance. One instance was his requirement that constables salute the chief, even when he, in his car, passed a beat constable out on the street. His reason was

Chief David Ritchie at Castle Mountain (now Mt. Eisenhower) in 1937. *(Photo: Calgary Police Service Archives)*

David Ritchie served as chief from 1919 until his death in 1941. *(Photo: Calgary Police Service Archives)*

that a constable, alert enough to spot the chief driving by, was alert enough to spot a wrongdoer.

Ritchie released four constables for street duty by hiring civilian males for such non-essential positions as his own secretary, and telephone switchboard operators who, by the way, he recruited from the ranks of disabled war veterans. The chief sought clear lines of authority and the naming of a deputy, Inspector Nutt being his choice. However for the next 30 years, because of the reluctance of city council, the second in command was variously referred to as "chief inspector" or "assistant chief" until, in 1947, the police commission authorized the appointment of a Deputy Chief of Police.

Chief David Ritchie was at the helm of the force through the devastating Depression of the 1930s and through some awkward "growing-pains" years as the automobile craze swept through the community. By 1920 Calgary, that had gawked at its first automobile in 1901, was chalking up more than two car accidents a day, about one hundred each month.

Calgary police in front of City Hall, approximately 1919.
(Photo: Calgary Police Service Archives)

A head-on collision between a car and a horse-drawn city watering cart became our worst accident of 1912, with the deaths of the automobile driver and his passenger. The community's first hit-and-run fatality to be investigated and docketed by the police happened in late September 1914 and, in January 1916, a young woman became Calgary's first motorist to be convicted of manslaughter. These

Chief Ritchie freed police manpower for outside duties after World War I by providing jobs to disabled war veterans. C. J. 'Rosie' O'Grady (left) and Marshal McDougall operated the call box signal system and switchboard for years, often in a very entertaining manner. *(Photo: courtesy Jack DeLorme and Harry Befus, Calgary Herald photographers)*

events, and local motorists' propensity for speeding, created a whole new dimension for the police. They had no effective means of clocking and apprehending reckless drivers. The department's only police car was used mainly by the chief, and mounted patrolmen were no match for speeders.

Accidents such as this one involving a Model T Ford occurred with increasing frequency as the number of automobiles on city streets grew.
(Photo: courtesy of the Glenbow Archives)

Calgary's love affair with the automobile started early in the 1900s. Mr. Lent, a city lawyer, promoted this parade of new automobiles in 1915.
(Photo: courtesy of the Provincial Archives of Alberta)

Consequently Chief Ritchie, in his annual report of 1920, strongly recommended "...that permission be granted for the purchase of at least two motorcycles, in order that the Department may effectively cope with this serious practice." So, in 1921 one specially-equipped Harley-Davidson was bought and immediately put to work, while the citizens' apprehensive term "motorcycle cop" entered our vocabulary.

Calgary police constables west of police headquarters in 1920.
(Photo: Calgary Police Service Archives)

Constable Rod Williamson was chosen for the job. He was the only member on the force who could ride the machine, having been a dispatch rider in the army overseas. With a top speed of 80 miles an hour the Harley and Williamson could nab a speeder without any trouble. The officer found Calgary's early motorists to be more polite and co-operative than the roads! Calgary streets and avenues, in the 1920s, were not extensively paved, street car tracks jutted ominously, and some hard surfacing was that of sandstone or cedar blocks that behaved very restlessly under the influence of frost and heavy rain.

Rod Williamson had one nasty spill when his motor bike's front wheel lodged in the 9th Avenue East street car track. That sudden unscheduled stop cost the constable three hospitalized days of unconsciousness. Williamson's speeder-apprehending technique was very effective. He gave habitual offenders two warnings, noting their names and addresses in his "black book" for his own

Crews at work paving 8 Avenue in November 1908. The paving material here appears to be wooden blocks, which were notorious for their reaction to rain and frost.
(Photo: courtesy of Duke Kent)

Two new Harley-Davidson motorcycles appear in this photo of the 1924 Calgary Police Uniform Department. The officer on the motorcycle to the left is Constable Rod Williamson, Calgary's first motorcycle officer. His diplomacy in checking speeders eased the acceptance of the motorcycle as a law enforcement tool by Calgary motorists.
(Photo: Calgary Police Service Archives)

information. The third time was the one that hurt because it meant a court appearance and a fine.

The motorcycle patrol, skimpy as it was, met with such success that in 1924 the old machine was retired and replaced by two new models, each with a sidecar. In a cost-saving move the horse patrol was disbanded and by 1927 the force was using two motorcycles on patrol by day and one by night.

Automobile driver licences were not introduced in Alberta until 1929 so prior to that time it was hard for police to keep track of reckless motorists. Moreover, it was possible for persuasive and well-heeled wrongdoers behind the wheel to try paying the patrolman the

City police tug o'war team, 1924. Seated at left is Chief D. Ritchie; at right is Inspector W. A. Nutt.
(Photo: Calgary Police Service Archives)

fine at the scene of the misdemeanour. The time had come for written traffic tickets.

Chief Ritchie instituted a system of 20-minute parking in such congested areas as 8th Avenue, and colored traffic tickets: pink for a vehicle shortcoming such as a broken headlight or missing licence plate; blue for such traffic infractions as overdue and careless parking. With very few sedan cars in those days, the traffic ticket was left hanging on the steering wheel, because not all vehicles had windshield wipers. The fine was $1.00, and the first ticket was issued on January 12, 1921.

Class of 1929 outside police headquarters.
(Photo: Calgary Police Service Archives)

Before long it was obviously necessary that the ticket design should be revised to include details of the infraction and the badge number of the officer who had tagged the car. In those early days of ticketing the novelty caught the imagination of passing youngsters who found it fun to move a tag from one parked vehicle to another. At a later date it became necessary to imprint the traffic ticket with the city insignia to discourage a prankish citizen from causing a bit of turmoil by tagging unoffending cars with counterfeit tags of his own making.

A good many of today's motorists might welcome that sort of a chuckle in the light of the solemn dedication of the do-it-to-the-letter-by-the-book of the Canadian Corps of Commissionaires who, in 1953, took over the job of issuing parking tags.

As the Depression deepened there was growing restlessness among the unemployed. The city was drowning in debt, occasioned in large part by the payout of relief to the jobless. One immediate saving was to be the discontinuance of relief payments to jobless

1929 Police Department in front of police headquarters.
(Photo: Calgary Police Service Archives)

Calgary's detectives pose outside police headquarters in 1928.
(Photo: Calgary Police Service Archives)

single men. Immediately the police were faced with about 2,000 protesters who, despite their lack of a parade permit, were marching through town.

There was a free-for-all between the jobless and a police squad led by sergeants Cox and Millan. A blow to the head hospitalized Millan and the protest leaders were hailed into court. There, Detective Sergeant Joe Carruthers found one of the spectators carrying a loaded gun and swiftly took the man into custody.

This photograph of the 1932 Calgary police revolver team nicely illustrates the variety of uniforms then in use. Uniforms of the senior officers (chief constable and inspector) are seen at far left and far right respectively. In the center is the khaki uniform worn by the motorcycle detail. This uniform is said to have been adopted because it did not show road dust as easily as dark blue tunics. The others in the photo are wearing what were then the familiar dark blue, high-necked tunics and 'bobby' style helmets of beat constables and their sergeants. Also note the variety of hat badges shown here.
(Photo: Calgary Police Service Archives)

Financial assistance was announced by the federal government but a few weeks later, in the summer of 1931, city council voted to require each unemployed man to work two days, rather than one day a week, on a city project in order to qualify for relief. This decision did not sit at all well with the National Unemployed Workers' Association. It urged its many followers to go on strike and another crowd assembled to march on City Hall.

These ones were met by Chief Ritchie who advised them to forget their parade and to gather instead on "Red Square," a vacant lot not far from the Communist Party's headquarters on 8th Avenue East. But, he warned, once they had gathered there, inflammatory speeches were prohibited. However, when one of the leaders, Philip Luck, defied that ban, Sergeant Burroughs arrested him and "Red Square" became the site of another

During the Depression, Calgary was the scene of a number of marches by unemployed men. This one, shown moving along 2 Street East at 10 Avenue, occurred in 1932.
(Photo: courtesy of the Glenbow Archives)

fight. In this melee an Alberta Provincial Police constable was knocked out by a thrown brick and more arrests followed.

That night Ritchie's men raided the Communists' headquarters. Someone doused the lights while everyone mixed it up in the dark. When lighting was restored the police had the upper hand, but upon escorting their attackers out of the building the police were set upon by a large mob awaiting them. This time it was Sergeant Cox who took a cement block to the head followed immediately by a fast trip to the hospital. The explosive situation was defused when council hastily rescinded its two-day work requirement.

Things were desperate but comparatively quiet for some months until, in the spring of 1933, council felt compelled to cut relief costs by reducing the unemployment payment by 25%. By this time the Depression had become so awesome that only half the jobless had the spirit to go on strike. April 24, 1933 was the day planned by the strikers for a big demonstration. They resented the non-participation of about 70 workers on a project in the Mission district who were being given police protection while they stayed on the job.

The fuse was lit for another donnybrook and, sure enough, later in the day about 1,500 strikers attacked the police, sweeping them aside, injuring constables Rod Williamson and J.McRae. The police regrouped, kept the cat-calling strikers at bay, and regained control of the situation.

The following day Chief Ritchie, with the backing of Inspector Carruthers and five constables, again had to convince the angry strikers that a parade was out of the question. And again city council had to cancel its plan to invoke the 24% pay cut in order to restore some semblance of calm to the tense confrontation.

In the midst of these great difficulties the Calgary police received a heavy blow. Inspector Joe Carruthers, a member of the force for 21 years, was murdered on duty on the night of June 13, 1933. This very popular and highly-respected policeman, at the age of 46, was planning to marry and, in order to be assigned to the day shift following his wedding, he worked the night shift in June.

In the small hours of that Tuesday morning a police driver and Inspector Carruthers were driving detectives James McDonald and Tom Cassie home at the end of their shift. Carruthers had planned to make the rounds of other officers on duty before dawn. They stopped at a flashing call box to learn that a prowler had robbed a house in the Scarboro residential district. They sped to the scene and spotted someone ducking into a back lane.

Inspector Joe Carruthers was killed by an unknown assailant on June 13, 1933.
(Photo: Calgary Police Service Archives)

While the car circled the block, Detective Macdonald and Inspector Carruthers closed in on the suspect. Suddenly Carruthers was aiming his flashlight at the culprit's face. A single shot at point-blank range passed below his out-stretched arm that held the flashlight, and penetrated his heart, killing him almost instantly.

At the inquest it was determined that the weapon was a rusty .32 calibre Iver Johnson revolver using ammunition at least 20 years old. It was the sort of weapon often carried by transients. Despite a widespread and drawn-out search the culprit was not caught or identified. However, many years later the police announced Carruthers' murderer had been located in an institution for the criminally insane.

The large number of unemployed kept the police in a constant state of special alert, particularly when the jobless were required to work off part of their relief payments. A reduction of relief allotments in 1938 resulted in some prickly situations when half the recipients worked while the other half went on strike, protesting with heckling, placards, meetings, and downtown marches.

In 1957 The Calgary Herald carried a story which indicated that a possible solution to the long-unsolved murder of Joe Carruthers had been found. *(Photo: Calgary Police Service Archives)*

By 1938 the unemployment rolls were shrinking as the trickle of jobs increased to a flow that swept Calgarians, weary of idleness, into the productive work stream. Matters eased for the men on the force such as Constable Rod Williamson. He was grateful for the upturn for he recalled, without pleasure, of having to meet trains of unemployed "riding the rods." One of his jobs was to march them to a soup kitchen then back to the rail yards to urge them to continue their hopeless quest for work somewhere else.

Williamson described his police career as **"...the most miserable job anybody can have."** Jack Smith, who became inspector, recalled 8-hour night shifts with a 20-minute meal break for a sandwich he carried in his pocket. Shortly after joining the force in the summer of 1930 he stopped on his beat to chat about his new job with some girls he knew. They thought he looked good in his new uniform and told him so and the flattered rookie dallied too long. He did not know his sergeant had reported him for gossiping for which "sin" he was fined two days' pay!

When Chief Ritchie had held the post for 20 years he asked the police commission for replacement of the antiquated 1914 communication system and for additions to the 2-car prowler "fleet." Opposition came from Alderman H.R.Chauncey, a jeweller whose store robbery in the early 1920s had never been solved. Chauncey believed crime existed only in the 20-block downtown core area which required neither prowler cars nor beat policemen. However the commission overruled the jeweller, stating that **"Calgary has one of the most efficient police departments in Canada. It is well disciplined and, from the chief constable down, is doing an excellent job with the means at its disposal."**

M.J. 'Duke' Kent (left) and Jimmy Steele in their greatcoats in December of 1937. The coats were anything but 'great,' however, because they were worn over the holster like a tent and were cold.

(Photo: courtesy of Duke Kent)

To underline its endorsement council approved the purchase and installation of a 60-watt Marconi 3-way radio system linking headquarters and two motorcycle and four automobile patrols on roving assignments throughout town. Another valuable addition to the lawmen's "tools of the trade" was a laboratory staffed by assistant city chemist J.W. Young and Detective Larry S. Partridge. These were timely moves inasmuch as in May 1939 Their Majesties King George VI and Queen Elizabeth arrived in Calgary on their continent-wide tour.

Mayor Andy Davidson and Chief D. Ritchie greet King George VI and Queen Elizabeth on their royal visit to Canada in 1939. Shortly after their return to England, World War II broke out in Europe.
(Photo: Calgary Police Service Archives)

Their stay was brief but, under Chief Ritchie's command, some 4,000 uniformed personnel from the Canadian Army, RCMP, Post Office Letter Carriers, and Legion of Frontiersmen augmented the roles of the City of Calgary Police in lining the 8-mile parade route, handling crowds of children and adults, ensuring safety of the royal visitors. It tested the mettle of all who took part in the once-in-a-lifetime experience, especially the police officers whose numbers soon were to be spread thinly.

When World War II broke out, many policemen in great part because of their backgrounds, were quick to answer the call of the armed forces. Well-trained constables and the new close communication facilities made it possible for the force to maintain a high degree of visibility and effectiveness despite its depleted ranks. A few rather cunning touches were added, such as the routine of going on duty. It had been customary for duty policemen to march from headquarters, each man peeling off to his beat as they paraded west on 7th Avenue. The chief instructed officers to leave headquarters by the back door in order not to reveal to the city's criminal element how lean the police ranks actually were!

This reassuring photo appeared in The Calgary Herald on June 17, 1942 when Calgary police were receiving training in the use of the tommy gun and Bren Gun, 'two of the Canadian (Active) Army's deadliest weapons.'
(Photo: courtesy of The Calgary Herald)

The early war years of 1940 and '41 dealt additional severe blows to the force. Constable John Crocker was killed in a flying accident; Constable Johnny Rogers was hospitalized due to two motorcycle accidents while on duty; Constable Wilf Cox lost his life while on motorcycle duty. In June 1941 Calgarians were shocked to learn that Chief Ritchie, while undergoing gall bladder surgery, died on a hospital operating table.

There was little time for mourning. A few days after the death of the chief, who had headed the force for almost 22 years, Inspector Sam Patterson, a Calgary policeman for 28 years, was appointed head of the force. His was the responsibility of guiding the maintenance of law and order through the trying years of World War II, post-war years of adjustment and the catapulting of Calgary into a boom-town category with the major 1947 oil discovery.

This hitherto small and quite law-abiding city suddenly became headquarters of a host of petroleum exploration and development companies, home of many hundreds of United States oilmen and their families transferred here in order to bring their expertise to bear upon this province's fabulous new mineral bonanza.

Patterson, a big soft-spoken Irishman, was well suited for times of great change. The force he had inherited from Chief Ritchie had fewer than 70 people, an even smaller group of law enforcers than the city had known at the start of World War I. It had to be augmented. As discharged armed forces' personnel became available, hiring began anew, with some recruits replacing grey-headed police veterans who had been re-hired during the wartime manpower shortage.

Samuel Patterson was chief from 1941 to 1950. *(Photo: Calgary Police Service Archives)*

Sam Patterson's most newsworthy undertaking was his addition of women to the police force. Prior to 1939 the police matron was the only woman on strength, for in those earlier days even secretaries and clerks were male. Yet as far back as 1912 women's groups had agitated for the addition of women to the force. In the days of Chief Cuddy city council made provision for the appointment of a woman detective but the chief was stubborn: **"As for women detectives or police officers, we have no need whatever for them...."**

So it remained for Chief Patterson, a quarter of a century later, to hire Vera Russell, Margaret Sadler, O.C."Cubby" Stanton, and Nora Peavoy as Calgary's first women police officers. Two civilian secretaries were hired, Mona Bailey being the first, and to every man's surprise things worked out very well once the initial week or so of awkwardness was surmounted. The men in blue, who had sort of tiptoed around the situation on their best behaviour, soon loosened up and discovered the women to be willing and capable working partners.

Officers Russell and Stanton were replaced in time by Magdalene Hettler and Isa Buccini, who remained on the force for 12 years at which time Sadler left to marry Detective Gordon Gilkes. Describing in later years what it had been like at the first, Margaret Gilkes remembered: **"Certainly women could not carry billy, handcuffs or gun. Driving prowler cars was out of the question although Stanton and I had been transport drivers in the army as well as being trained and experienced with pistol, rifle and shotgun.**

Three of the first policewomen on the Calgary police payroll were: Margaret Sadler (above left); R. 'Cubby' Stanton (above right) shown here in a 1946 photo; and Vera Russell (whose photo appears below).
(Photo: reproduced by Glenbow Archives)

"The new policewomen were outfitted in navy blue uniforms with skirts resting demurely about mid-calf; pork pie hats similar to the type worn by the V.O.N. except with Calgary Police hat badges; heavy black oxfords, white shirts and black ties; heavy navy blue greatcoats with the city police insignia on the shoulder; and navy blue trench coats."

Vera Russell
(Photo: Calgary Police Service Archives)

This 1958 photograph shows four policewomen. Isa Buccini (left) was taken on strength in 1949. The other three (left to right), Marg Sadler, O.C. Stanton, and Nora Peavoy, were taken on strength in 1945.
(Photo: Calgary Police Service Archives)

Policewomen Buccini and Sadler in a posed picture, shown escorting a 'prisoner' into the charge office of police headquarters.
(Photo: Calgary Police Service Archives)

The women were given no beat, just expected to patrol wherever they felt they could do the most good. At one point Gilkes confronted a pair of burly men outside the Ritz Hotel. Unarmed of course, she instructed them to accompany her to headquarters. They bolted and she chased, unsuccessfully. Her sergeant asked dryly, "What would you have done if you had caught them?" Gilkes had no answer but her suspicions and alertness were justified when later in the day the men were apprehended. They had been loaded with about $1,000 worth of stolen jewelery when she first accosted them.

When Chief Patterson retired in June 1950 after 9 years at the helm, the force numbered 147 including 4 policewomen and a civilian staff of 21, many of whom were women. Having reached pensionable age, he said of his historical decision: "I cannot overlook the Policewomen of the Department. To them I would like to express my thanks for the tactful and quiet way they have always accomplished a difficult task."

During his tenure as chief, Sam Patterson made a pair of important changes, one of them occasioned by the increasing mechanization of the force. The helmet type of headgear was impractical for those in prowler cars, so the forage cap was adopted. The traditional high-necked tunic was replaced by open jacket, shirt and tie.

The other innovation was the creation of a traffic division headed by Sergeant Chris Stagg. Until 1950 those officers handled jobs normally done by traffic engineers: erecting "No Parking" and "Stop" signs, and Stagg even recalled occasions when he and his men went out late at night to paint crosswalks! Another of their tasks, beginning in 1948, was ensuring motorists were not forgetting to feed the 580 new downtown parking meters.

One of Chief Patterson's inheritances of the 1940s was the city police School Safety Patrol. It began as an idea in the mind of the traffic unit's Sergeant Bill Eager who, in 1937, was concerned for the safety of small school children crossing busy roads on their way to and from class. Eager held meetings with parents, teachers, and students that resulted in the first patrol being tried out at Balmoral High School in January 1938.

It was an instant success and during that year, patrols, supervised by 141 students, were established on busy thorough-fares outside 15 other city schools. By then, Sergeant Rod Williamson, the police contact with schools, felt that busy as they were, the traffic unit should help the patrol system achieve a higher degree of public attention.

Detective Inspector Reg
Clements in his office, 1948.
*(Photo: courtesy of the Glenbow
Archives)*

Temporary detective office in
the parade room at
headquarters in 1948. (Left to
right: Jack Smith; Duke Kent;
Mona Bailey).
*(Photo: courtesy of the Glenbow
Archives)*

Interior of detective front
office in 1948. Left to right
are: Mona Bailey; Reg
Clements; Warren Stewart;
Bruce McCannel; Jack Smith.
*(Photo: Courtesy of the Glenbow
Archives)*

Interior of detective office in
1948. Left to right are Kay
Hodges and Andy Hendry.
*(Photo: courtesy of the Glenbow
Archives)*

The Identification Section's
fingerprint and photo file
room at police headquarters.
*(Photo: Calgary Police Service
Archives)*

In 1951 part of the hazards of
winter driving were frosty
windows. The plastic stick-on
window panels didn't help
much.
*(Photo: Calgary Police Service
Archives)*

Sergeant Bill Eager founded
the School Safety Patrol
Program in 1938, when a
patrol was formed at Balmoral
School.
*(Photo: Calgary Police Service
Archives)*

Don Hanson leading the
Calgary School Patrol Band.
*(Photo: Calgary Police Service
Archives)*

Instead of patrollers making their
own cloth belts, professionally-made
belts and badges were provided by the
Alberta Motor Association. "Courtesy
Versus Death," a traffic education
series aimed at motorists, became a
regular radio feature, and Chris Stagg
put Don Hanson in charge of traffic
education. Thousands of school
children got to know Hanson who
helped organize the "Safety Round-
Up" television series whose student
band travelled across Canada giving
public performances. In 1964, in recog-
nition of his splendid work, Sergeant
Hanson was named Calgary's Citizen
of the Year.

The Traffic Education Unit was an
excellent undertaking for its high-
profile work helped create a valuable
new relationship between citizens and
their police. Each became increasingly
aware of the other's concerns and
problems and, as Ed Madsen discovered when he was posted to Traffic
Education, defensive attitudes arising
from suspicion of one another's behaviour markedly diminished.

Between May 1950 and April 1952
four police chiefs came and went, all
good men but all holding the position
briefly on their threshold of retirement.
It was a time of moderate civic growth

The Calgary Safety Roundup
Band and Singers,
accompanied by Don Hanson,
appeared on Parliament Hill
in 1962.
(Photo: courtesy of Apex Photos,
Ottawa)

The Calgary Safety Roundup television program was popular in Calgary in the
early 1960s.
(Photo: Calgary Police Service Archives)

School patrollers at work in 1965 under the guidance of a constable from the Traffic Education Unit.
(Photo: Calgary Police Service)

but there was agitation for an overdue improvement in the pay scale for a chief and, for the force, younger dynamic leadership.

On July 1, 1952 another internal appointment was made when Inspector Larry Partridge was named Calgary's chief constable on the understanding that the police commission was looking to him for some significant organizational changes. Partridge had intended to follow his English father into the medical profession but a desire for overseas adventure brought him to Calgary as a recruit beat policeman in 1926. Upon completing his climb through the ranks, Partridge set himself the task of examining several urban forces in Canada and the United States on site. Based upon those findings he made three recommendations: (1) every police unit should be under a senior officer's command; (2) a homicide squad should be created within the detectives' office; (3) a program of training courses should be given everyone, from recruits to senior officers.

Chief Partridge, right from the start, was determined to have city council approve a new police headquarters building. On June 21, 1961 the new long-delayed facility was officially opened at 316 7th Avenue S.E. The 3-storey building, designed to carry 3 additional floors at a later date, provided a most welcome and sorely-needed 70,000 square feet of working space and cells for 100 prisoners. However, in less than ten years facilities again were strained to the limit and not until mid-June 1976 were they enlarged.

Swifter than his efforts to achieve adequate headquarters was Partridge's success in forming, in late 1952, the homicide unit. Led

Malcolm Boyd was
chief from June 27 to
September 29, 1950.
*(Photo: Calgary Police
Service Archives)*

Reg Clements held the
position of chief from
September 29, 1950 to
September 17, 1951.
*(Photo: Calgary Police Service
Archives)*

James McDonald, who was
chief from 1951 to April of
1952, was the fourth man to
hold the position in two years.
*(Photo: Calgary Police Service
Archives)*

Constable L.
Partridge's
first day on
the job, 1926.
*(Photo: Calgary
Police Service
Archives)*

Larry Partridge slowed the
turnover in chiefs by
remaining in the position from
1952 until 1964.
*(Photo: Calgary Police Service
Archives)*

Constable
L.Partridge,
approximately
1930.
*(Photo: Calgary
Police Service
Archives)*

Detective
Partridge in his
office, 1930s.
*(Photo: Calgary
Police Service
Archives)*

Constable A. Anderson on the police switchboard, approximately 1953.
(Photo: Calgary Police Service Archives)

In the 1950s the Calgary Stampede commenced on Mondays. Calgarians who couldn't wait for the fun to start often began on Sunday night in the downtown area. Police were there to ensure everyone had a reasonable amount of fun.
(Photo: Calgary Police Service Archives)

Traffic Squad in front of the police garage in 1954.
(Photo: Calgary Police Service Archives)

Renovations to police garage, with patrol cars in front, 1956-57. *(Photos: courtesy Tom Gummo)*

by Detective Sergeant M.J.Kent, with member detectives M.G.Higgett, I.G.Gilkes, and K.W.Evans, before three months had passed these experts were working on their first murder. Calgary had become a big city with a population approaching 150,000 and the need for greater police specialization was becoming increasingly

The official opening of the new Calgary police building took place on June 21, 1961. Left to right: Chief L. Partridge; Mayor H. Hays; Alberta Premier E.C. Manning; and M.L.A. Art Dixon.
(Photo: courtesy Duke Kent)

The new police headquarters building was completed in 1961.
(Photo: Calgary Police Service Archives)

With the new police building open just down the street, the old building at 333 - 7 Avenue S.W. was torn down in 1962.
(Photo: Calgary Police Service Archives)

Detective Sergeant Malcolm J. Kent examines a slide prior to insertion in a comparison microscope in the Hair and Fiber Section of the FBI laboratory. Kent graduated with the 50th session of the FBI National Academy on November 14, 1952.
(Photo: Calgary Police Service Archives)

apparent. By 1955 Chief Partridge had come up with a plan to completely reorganize the force.

The 12 police beats, established in 1930 and unchanged since then, were increased to 20. Patrol cars were assigned to residential areas, thus being readily available everywhere in the expanding city. The painstaking and detailed checking of office and warehouse property became the beat constables' responsibility throughout each night. The force was re-framed into four branches, resulting in promotions to new positions.

Emerging from this reorganization was Deputy Chief Ken McIver who had charge of the detective branch. Chief Inspector Jock Ritchie headed the patrol branch. Inspector Chris Stagg ran the traffic branch and Inspector Malcolm "Duke" Kent was responsible for developing training and refresher courses.

Long before Larry Partridge came on the Calgary police scene 4 sub-stations had been opened in 1912 in

Homicide training exercises
provided police officers with
the techniques they would call
upon in their work with the
Homicide Unit.
(Photo: courtesy the Albertan)

Matching fingerprints was
often a tedious,
time-consuming job.
*(Photo: Calgary Police Service
Archives)*

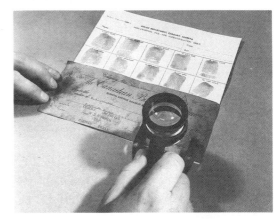

The Identification Section
darkroom as it appeared in
1956.
*(Photo: Calgary Police Service
Archives)*

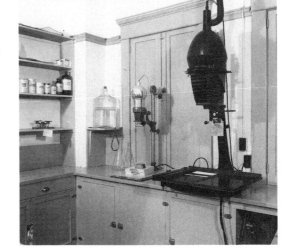

In 1950 the preferred headgear for detectives seems to have been the fedora hat. Within the group seen here are five men who would eventually succeed Malcolm Boyd (front row, fourth from left) as chief.
(Photo: Calgary Police Service Archives)

order to base groups of officers close to the community need. The idea was premature for they lasted only two years before being labelled extravagant. Chief Partridge, well after his time, in the mid 1980s would heartily have approved the establishment of 6 district offices, effectively distributing the capability of the force throughout the ever-growing sprawl of our city of 650,000.

As Calgary grew, so the problems attendant upon a larger, closely-knit urban community multiplied, along with the need for administering an increasingly-complex police system. The practice of having the mayor as chairman of the Police Committee fortunately had long been abandoned. Then for decades a police commission composed of three aldermen had been quite adequate. Political pressures of the 1930s, though, forced a decision to remove the police force from council's control.

By an amendment to the city charter a Calgary Police Commission board was created. Membership was defined as a senior judge of the district court, a senior police magistrate, the mayor as board chairman, and a senior police officer as secretary. During the ensuing years changes were considered but not enacted until, in 1956,

This newspaper ad announcing career opportunities with the Calgary City Police appeared in 1956. Although women had been with the city police since 1945, advertising was still aimed at men. *(Photo: Calgary Police Service Archives)*

Career Opportunities with

CALGARY CITY POLICE

If you want a man's job . . . a job that is truly important . . . you'll find it with Calgary's police. Never before has the police force offered so many career opportunities for specialization and advancement. Constables' starting salary is $246.00 per month, rising to $322.00 in 3 years. Three weeks' annual leave and pension on completion of service.

ARE YOU a British subject between 19 and 25 years old (up to 30 years with Armed Forces service), not less than 5' 10" in height, with good health, sound basic education and good character? Then . . . write for application form to:

CHIEF OF POLICE, **CITY POLICE BUILDING**
Calgary, Alberta

Weather has always added to the rigors of walking a beat, as this photo of two officers working through a snowstorm in 1956 illustrates. *(Photo: courtesy of the Calgary Herald)*

Auto accidents, then as now, often required quick action on the part of police. *(Photo: Calgary Police Service Archives)*

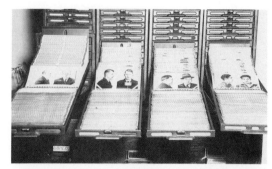

Photo files maintained by the
Identification Section.
*(Photo: Calgary Police Service
Archives)*

Sergeant Ernie Hetherington
and recruits look on as a
trainee takes aim, 1956.
*(Photo: Calgary Police Service
Archives)*

Inspector 'Duke' Kent stands
behind Recruit Class #8 in a
training room at the old police
building in 1958.
*(Photo: Calgary Police Service
Archives)*

Sergeant Ernie Hetherington
shows a member of the 1959
recruit class the layout.
*(Photo: courtesy Ron Meigh,
Calgary Herald)*

Motorcycles at the Jubilee
Auditorium, approximately
1960.
*(Photo: Calgary Police Service
Archives)*

City workers remove a call box standard
from its location at 8 Avenue and 4 Street
S.W. Police personnel had no regrets when
this system was slowly dismantled starting
in the late 1960s.
(Photo: Calgary Police Service Archives)

Constable Joe Sitter at a
call box.
*(Photo: Calgary Police
Service Archives)*

the membership was altered to consist of the mayor, the senior police magistrate, two aldermen, and a Calgary representative of the bar association.

Switchboards at the new police building, 1961.
(Photo: Calgary Police Service Archives)

Dispatching calls, 1961.
(Photo: Calgary Police Service Archives)

Ten years later the police commission was freed of all political and outside pressures and charged with the responsibility of the appointment, control, direction, supervision, discipline, and governing of the force. Late in the 1960s the non-traditional style of Mayor Rod Sykes broke the more-than-80-year pattern of the mayor's role in police matters. For a while this caused a serious rift in commission-police relations that resulted in an inquiry and subsequent amendments to the Police Act.

Today's Municipal Police Commission must consist of three persons designated by the Attorney General of Alberta in consultation with the mayor, and two members of the municipal council, neither of whom can be named chairman. The group's secretary must be an employee of the commission, not a senior police officer.

The commission's work is not easy, for members must be sensitive to the wishes of citizens as well as of council and of police. The citizen and aldermanic members must be diligent to ensure the police are free of political pressures and responsive to community concerns. This stance is inevitable in

Communications.
(Photo: Calgary Police Service Archives)

a typical complex society and community such as the Calgary of today. The simplicity of our yesterdays is gone forever even though so short a time has passed since our first chief constable, Jack S.Ingram, had to solve the knotty problem of creating a town jail.

A small cottage had been rented from Tom McHugh as a town hall. The mounties at the fort refused to hold drunks and rowdies in their jail so Ingram was compelled to negotiate with McHugh for new accommodation. By raising the monthly rent on the "Town Hall" from $15 to $20, the landlord agreed to build a small lockup out at the back. It ended up as a 16-foot-square solid log jail with 8-foot walls, a 2-inch thick door with a lock, and iron bars at the windows.

Council did some fast number work and decided it would be cheaper to own than to rent. So it took only six months to begin construction on a new 2-storey building containing town offices, a police station, and 3 jail cells. Meanwhile the rented jail was never divided into cells, creating another headache for the police chief but bringing in extra revenue for the town.

As the Herald newspaper of June 4, 1885 reported: **"Now that prisoners have come to consider the municipal lock-up a place to exercise their ingenuity on, rather than a place of confinement — three prisoners having broken out of it last week — the municipal fines are showing a handsome increase since prisoners are now fined for smashing the corporation property in addition to their other offenses."**

What a difference a century makes! The sharp contrasts with such simple, uncluttered decisions and actions appear each time the force is confronted with new challenges. It was in Chief Partridge's time that the need was faced for such specializations as a Canine Patrol, and a Search and Rescue Unit.

Fred Moore, Harold Wake, Ian MacDonald, and Ken McNeil were the first to work with dogs in May 1960. They boarded in their own homes the dogs they handled and took them with them in regular patrol cars with a sheet of canvas to protect the back seat from dirty pawprints. At one point they discovered they had a very unofficial assistant in a notorious alcoholic nicknamed Pee Wee Falls.

First members of the Canine Unit (left to right): Constable Fred Moore with Ember; Constable Harold Wake with Dante; Constable Ian MacDonald with Spook; Constable Ken McNeil with Duke.
(Photo: Calgary Police Service Archives)

Constables MacDonald, Wake, and Moore were training 4-legged police recruits on the North Hill Shopping Centre's parking lot. Dogs were being trained to attack a "culprit" wearing a large padded arm protector. Out of nowhere reeled Pee Wee in his usual state, insisting he be allowed to play the role of the bad guy. So the sleeve was strapped to his arm but one of the dogs, possibly a teetotaler, refused to attack. At Constable Wake's urging another dog leaped at Pee Wee and knocked him violently to the ground.

As he lay there with the dog over him, Pee Wee burst into tears. The constables rushed across, fearing the attack had injured him. But the tears flowed only because, in being upended by the dog, Pee Wee's new mickey of whiskey had shattered. The only way the officers could stanch the tears was to replace the bottle. Whereupon Pee Wee spread the word around the east end of town that he was the one who had trained the police K-9 dogs.

As with the Canine Unit men, who took on specialized work at no expense to the force, so the Search and Rescue team, at the outset in July 1961, supplied their own diving equipment. Organizing it were Walter Jackson, Don Claughton, Bob McIlhayga, Jim Beattie, Blake Green, Richard Porter, and Gerald Twa, all ardent scuba divers. Since that time it has become larger, and a busy part of police specialties.

Search and Rescue Unit equipment in the 1960s.
(Photo: Calgary Police Service Archives)

Not every man on the force is suited to special duties. In fact, not every recruit is necessarily good cop material. There was one young fellow posted to the traffic detail who specialized in tearing up the driver's license of an erring motorist he had pulled over for a minor infraction. Then he would tell him he could not proceed because he had no driver's licence. There was another who, between uniform beat duty, would don plain clothes and with his cuffs and gun out of sight stand outside the Queen's Hotel. He would nab emerging drunks, one

Search and Rescue Unit divers at work.
(Photo: Calgary Police Service Archives)

after another, and take them to headquarters, a "pastime" that did not sit well with his superiors.

One rookie posted himself at 9th Avenue and 12th Street East to stop motorists whose cars had a broken headlight or windshield wipers or other minor visible defect. He would direct each one to a corner service station with orders to remain there until the damage was repaired. It was a great

Policeman on point duty on Centre Street in the early 1900s.
(Postcard photo: Calgary Police Service Archives)

idea but it brought an official complaint from the service station attendant. He was on duty alone and could not possibly handle the flow of cars and angry drivers.

The first point duty assignment in Calgary was to direct traffic at 1st Street West and 8th Avenue. Retired Chief George Kemp and retired Deputy Chief Howard Leary recalled being relief men at that intersection when they were greenhorns. Each made the same mistake, not realizing that street cars were only inches apart when they made a turn at the same time. The veterans remembered fiendish gleams in the eyes of motormen who saw the oppor-

A policeman on point duty at 8 Avenue and 1 Street West, approximately 1926. Note the manually-operated 'Stop' and 'Go' sign.
(Photo: Calgary Police Service Archives)

tunity to trap a rookie policeman before the boys in blue wisely learned to wave only one car at a time through the turn!

Staff Sergeant Barrow's story, told on himself, is about his discovery that police recruits could not wear glasses. Barrow, who had worn them as a miner and in the Royal Canadian Navy, was stunned. But, being resourceful, he memorized the eye chart in the examination room. He passed with 20/20 vision even though he recited the chart exactly from the big "E" at the top, right through to the "Lithographed in Canada" in the bottom right-hand corner.

One of the least attractive police beats was No.20, usually called The Trapline because it required the constable to trudge out to the west edge of town adjoining the railway on 9th Avenue West. Occasionally a patrolling constable would encounter a skunk out there. Gerry Befus did, and had to take great care not to alarm it in case it made his long trek back to headquarters uncomfortable and unlovable!

One rookie, an ex-mountie, checked all points under his care on that walk west, then figured he might be able to hop a slow-moving morning freight for a free ride back into town. It was a great idea at 5 a.m. when he tried it, except that the train kept ambling through Calgary non-stop. As it passed the Palliser Hotel it began to gain speed. The officer was out in east Calgary before he was able to leap off the train and hurry back to headquarters to explain why he was bruised as well as late phoning in.

The matter of recruits' nationality was underlined when Chief Partridge was about to retire. During his 12 years at the helm he had been known to hire a number of men from his homeland of England. When it appeared that his deputy Ken McIvor would succeed him, a number of staffers assured their colleagues from Britain that hiring would change noticeably under a new Canadian chief from Saskatchewan.

The teasing prompted ex-Londoner Constable Ron Tarrant to write a Christmas card to himself in a self-addressed envelope. He mailed it overseas to a friend who promptly sent it back. One day after parade Tarrant read the newly-arrived card, then exclaimed, **"By Jove, my old boss, Chief Inspector Birmingham-Smith of Scotland Yard has accepted the position of chief here in Calgary. He's a jolly good chap. It'll be good to see him again!"**

With that, Tarrant pinned it to the bulletin board where the local boys read it and were speechless. Rumors abounded and someone let the Albertan newspaper know. A subsequent column read: **"Word has it that a man called Birmingham-Smith will be the new chief....Who is Birmingham-Smith?...He is the chief inspector of Scotland Yard retired. The word came in a Christmas card which read 'Merry Christmas. See you in June!' "**

The joke had gone far enough and the next issue of the staff magazine, **PATROL**, contained a cartoon depicting the funeral of Birmingham-Smith. That ended all speculation as to the next Calgary city police chief.

A surprise that was no joke happened to Tarrant in his rookie days. New recruits were placed on duty right away even though they were not immediately furnished with all items of equipment. However, when it was learned that recruit Tarrant had two years' experience on the London police force, he was promptly supplied with a gun and holster. He had neglected to inform the recruiting officers that London bobbies performed their duties unarmed. So he had the real thing while his inexperienced fellow recruits were issued only holsters that they stuffed with newspaper to give the impression of preparedness!

Ken McIver was chief from July 1964 until March 1968. *(Photo: Calgary Police Service Archives)*

Uniforms for rookies were not immediately forthcoming either and those were the days when nearly all police walked the beat. After a brief introduction on foot with the senior beat man, the rookie was sent out on his own. There being no such things as personal radios back then, the beat constable had to ring into headquarters from a sidewalk call box. The call had to be placed every hour although the constable had 15 minutes' leeway on either side of the hour. Woe betide him if he was in no trouble but failed to call in. The call box was a cop's life-line, as it were, his only means of summoning help, so the call-in discipline was strictly enforced.

One of the dangers the rookie faced was walking the beat the first few months without a uniform. Recruit Jack Lamont learned that in a hurry. Checking the doors of business premises late at night he found a grocery store door open. Suspecting a break and entry he went in to make a check of the darkened store. He was looking up the owner's phone number to urge him to come down and lock up the place when the light snapped on and Lamont was looking down the barrel of a shotgun.

The owner lived upstairs and upon hearing a noise crept down to the shop where he confronted this "prowler" in civilian clothes. Lamont had to do some fast talking to get out of that one! He thinks his life was saved by his fedora hat. Thanks, in part, to the movies it seemed most people knew that only detectives and rookies wore fedoras!

Rookies of especially large build, such as young Constable Norman Lund, were able to acquit themselves physically, even if not sartorially! He became embroiled in many a fight he tried to break up outside some east-end hotels. Soon he smartened up by standing across the street at bar-closing time. The imbibers would tumble out and start trying to demolish one another. When he figured the combatants were nearing exhaustion, Lund would cross the street and sort out the tangle.

He knew ranch hands made it into Calgary two or three times a year, expecting to drink too much and get into the odd scrap. In Lund's estimation, they were rowdy but not deserving of arrest, except one who Constable Lund tried escorting to headquarters down the alley behind the Queen's and Imperial hotels. Suddenly this big and adequately intoxicated man realized what was happening to him. He hit Lund, then grabbed the constable by the chest, ripping off uniform, shirt, everything. They wrestled, and fortunately when Lund was finally on top, along came two detectives in a car. They shouldered through the enthusiastically-cheering beery crowd and broke up the "party" by rescuing the hard-pressed Lund before any blood was shed!

As for the younger element, if a constable came across a kid doing something really stupid, often he would rough him up a bit and take him home. Likely the father would take over and the matter would be dropped. Many a basically well-intentioned youngster would decide one run-in with a beat police constable was intimidating enough to make the straight and narrow seem pretty attractive. The courts did not have to become involved, the police having quietly nipped a potential problem in the bud.

Cop, Flatfoot, Bull, or The Law, whatever rather disrespectful name he endured, the beat policeman generally was known to the people among whom he walked, and was regarded as a pretty good guy just doing his job. When Bill Morrison retired after 32 years on the force he estimated he had pounded a total beat of 85,000 miles, wearing out 64 pairs of boots in the process. No constable of today would ever walk that mileage. On wheels, he can cover the same distance in 2 years' service.

The pattern of today's policing certainly is based upon wheels, closely linked by radio, patterned by computer, aided by entirely new generations of electronic devices that, by yesterday's standards, are capable of performing miracles.

Calgary and its police force and services grew at phenomenal paces on the heels of the 1960s. Between 1960 and 1985 the city's population burst from 243,000 to 650,000, due in part to the annexation of surrounding communities. Forest Lawn on the eastern side was added in 1961 and to the west, Montgomery and Bowness in 1963 and 1964 — moves that added to Calgary's size and to the area requiring police coverage. They marked further steps in personnel expansion that inevitably took away some of that family intimacy within the force.

It was then that Constable Phil Crosby-Jones, aware of the growing need for effective internal communication, had rounded up the volunteer help of Ray Palardy, Ron Tarrant, Jim Wiersma, Bill Starke, Jim

Beecroft, Don Brestler, Kay Kittle, Lina Tarrant, Derek McCorquindale, Jack Taylor, and Don Nelson to help assemble and publish **PATROL**, the monthly department magazine whose first edition appeared in July 1962.

Patrol Magazine under production. Left to right: Myrna McRoberts; Sergeant E. Hetherington; and Constable Phil Crosby-Jones.
(Photo: Calgary Police Service Archives)

Canada's first polygraph was put to restricted use in 1964, the year a pair of hand-held walkie-talkie radios was purchased and put into service with notable success on stake-out and special-assignment duty. Those radios were the forerunners of the increasingly-miniaturized "tools of the trade" that were destined to render obsolete even the once-essential street-corner call boxes.

Members of the Traffic Section pose for the last time in their khaki uniforms. In 1962 a change to dark blue uniforms was made.
(Photo: Calgary Police Service Archives)

The mid 1960s were years of increasing public questioning of established authority. Chief McIvor, knowing Calgarians were no exception to a developing trend, shrewdly and quietly put together a riot squad under the command of the department disciplinarian, Sergeant Major Hetherington. Because of the city's growing size and law-enforcement problems, there was a continuing need for additional men. Modern though the scene was, the old-fashioned practice of walking a beat was still used as a method of testing the mettle of recruits.

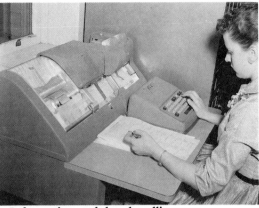

Information and data handling was becoming more sophisticated, as demonstrated in this photo showing the use of an IBM key punch machine in 1962.
(Photo: Calgary Police Service Archives)

With most of the force on wheels, foot patrols bore a bit of a stigma and became a training ground without a teacher. Inspec-

Clive Lee transporting children at the 1966 Stampede.
(Photo: Calgary Police Service Archives)

tor Fisher recalled a somewhat strange but usually effective training procedure. A rookie with recruiting school training but no beat experience was paired with a rookie who had pounded the pavement but had not yet been to recruiting school. Although it seemed like a case of the blind leading the blind while they made mistakes together, the scheme worked, perhaps because a seasoned officer usually was not too far away to help ensure the same errors were not repeated.

Bill Crabbe recalled one of his earlier foot patrols as a constable. At the corner of 23rd Avenue and 4th Street West in the Mission district he found the door of Avalon Cleaners slightly ajar. Stepping into the inky blackness of the place he came face-to-face with three people. "Hold it right there!" he yelled as he pulled his gun. "Anybody moves and I shoot!" They froze. Crabbe reached for his flashlight, snapped the switch, and found himself confronting three mannequins.

In later years these one-time greenhorns have relished telling stories of their days as red-hot rookies. Constable Hautzinger was patrolling a dark northeast alley in the small hours of the morning. Nothing disturbed the apparent peace and silence until he went through a high gate to check the back of a restaurant. As he pushed the gate, a cat that had been sleeping on top of it lost its balance, tumbled down Hautzinger's coat, clawing the front of it as it fell. Luckily the very startled constable did not shoot because, where the equally terrified cat clung, Hautzinger may have done some additional quite irreparable personal damage!

Most of the police sergeants of the mid 1960s were veterans of World War II, well versed in disciplinary lore. One of them would balance a penny on each of several remote doorknobs by way of testing if a rookie constable had indeed checked doors twice during the night. In the morning he would make a personal retrieval of undisturbed pennies in an attempt to catch the recruit in a matter of carelessness at the cost of a reprimand or a day's pay; or of dismissal in the case of an outright lie.

Pranks, while frowned upon by some, had their uses, for a sleepy or careless constable was vulnerable and could end up in deep trouble. New beat constables were at the mercy of the prowler-car crews until they picked up some of the "street smarts" that might, in some tight situation, be a lifesaver.

One favorite stunt involved a car crew befriending a foot-patrolling rookie on a very cold night. Once in the car the grateful new man would be told they had to look in on some troublemakers. They would ask him to help out by checking the back lane while they cased the front of the place. Of course when he returned to the front of the premises the patrol car would be gone, leaving the rookie to face a cold trip back to headquarters while, as required, reporting in regularly. Even the most naive newcomer to the force soon learned not to trust anyone until he really got to know them.

A greenhorn might find the silence of a black alley suddenly exploding with noise and light. It would just be a car crew flying down the alley for fun, testing his coolness and reflexes. But every month the shifts changed, constables were posted to other parts of the city and the "war" between a constable and a prowler-car pair could break out anew. However, because of this, many young constables quickly learned to be sensitive at all times to anything out of the ordinary.

Deputy Chief Ed Madsen, who was on the street for 3 years on a beat and 4 in a car, theorized that a good constable develops a sixth sense giving him a gut feeling that something is wrong. When he checks, 9 times out of 10, he is proven correct and is already alert to making a necessary arrest. When theory has to be translated into practical performance many more components are required in addition to gut feelings for, to an ever-increasing extent, science is essential to the success of the complex role of today's policeman.

The growth of the force, coupled with rapidly changing public mores in a complicated society, tend to make great demands upon those charged with the administration of the force. With the retirement of Chief McIver slated for early 1968 a search was begun for a successor. Then, for the first time in the history of the force a native-born Calgarian was appointed to the post. Next Chief Malcolm "Duke" Kent was given another southern Albertan as his right-

M.J. 'Duke' Kent was chief
from February 1968 to August
1972.
*(Photo: Calgary Police Service
Archives)*

Constable Kent at a church
parade in 1938. The white
helmet was considered
summer dress.
(Photo: courtesy Duke Kent)

Constable Duke Kent with car #4 in the
mid-1940s.
(Photo: courtesy Duke Kent)

hand man, popular ex-Stampeder and native of Lethbridge, Gordon Gilkes.

They had worked most of their uniformed lives together, were excellent team men, and soon were hard at work trying to instil that spirit and enthusiasm into a police force that had grown so large it was difficult to maintain any sort of close touch. The traditional system of maintaining internal discipline was not as healthy as it should be, as was the state of communication between the public and the police. Articulate senior officers such as Inspector Andy Little and Warrant Officer Art Roberts were booked to address various city groups but they were able to do little more than to give audiences the police view of what was wrong with the public.

One of Chief Kent's big problems was getting a handle on his own administration for by 1968 the force numbered 531 police and 73 civilians. Under the Straight Watch system that had not been changed in decades, any constable could be posted to any part of the city on any shift almost on a day-to-day basis. Keeping track of individuals' whereabouts, court time, days off, annual leave, was an administrative nightmare consuming hours of paperwork and, of course, making requests for switching duty highly unpopular.

In 1968 Chief Kent inaugurated a 5-platoon system. Each of 4 platoons was made up of a station sergeant, 3 patrol sergeants, a jailer, an assistant jailer, a dispatcher, an operator, a matron, and 61 constables for car and beat duty. The fifth platoon was composed of headquarters staff.

This unitizing and delegating of authority resulted in boosted morale as constables became familiar with other members of the platoon. In fact, spirited inter-platoon sports programs developed. However, the system's drawback was that a constable's particular posting would last only one month before he was rotated to another part of the city. This diminished an officer's sense of responsibility to a particular area and its problems, for he knew he would soon be moving elsewhere.

Constable Alexander Max received a prize from Chief Duke Kent in 1969 for his inspired motto, 'Chosen to Serve.' This motto is still used by the Calgary Police Service.
(Photo: Calgary Police Service Archives)

Although in-service training was increased, upper management still had little contact with recruits. The practice of hiring a lot of new men then over the next year or so weeding out the unsuitable ones, was an approach that begged correction. Crime-related courses for those confirmed in their positions covered counterfeiting, explosives, homicide, breathalyzer testing, and traffic investigation. All constables were trained in mob-control tactics, using new riot-squad equipment such as tear gas, smoke bombs, gas masks, plastic shields, riot sticks, and helmets.

Little drug-free Calgary had grown up, inheriting the roster of modern sins, so it was time an undercover drug unit was added to the force. It had to be more than a couple of men in fedoras and trench coats, too! Actually the first two on the detail, Boyd Davidson and Ian MacDonald, were assigned to work with a couple of RCMP drug specialists who had the job of laying most of the charges. By 1970 Jack Taylor and Don Mount replaced them, working principally in and around high schools.

The illegal drug trade in town continued to expand so, in 1971, a formal Drug Squad was created under the leadership of Sergeant of Detectives Al Menzies. The first course on drug control ever held in Canada took place at the Banff School of Fine Arts with instructors from the U.S. Federal Bureau of Narcotics and Dangerous Drugs. In attendance were Calgary officers Jack O'Neill, Bob Short, Jim Beattie, Ron Tarrant, Jack Taylor, Doug Green, Jeannie Blackie, and Joanne Budd, the 9 assigned to the squad.

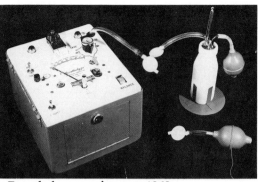
Breathalyzer equipment, 1968.
(Photo: Calgary Police Service Archives)

Sergeant Bill Wiste demonstrates control techniques to a training class in 1969.
(Photo: The Albertan)

Doug Green made one bust when posing as a postman. He made a house delivery of a slab of hash that had been spotted at the customs office. Then Green hung around while inside the house one of two brothers argued that the postman was too big and, besides, a postal delivery after 6 o'clock was a bit fishy. Green kicked the door open so that he could arrest the pair and confirm the fellow's suspicions.

Jim Beattie turned out to be one of the few policemen ever to see a dealer "capping up" — transferring bulk MDA into capsules. He lay on his tummy peering through the basement window of a house watching a young fellow making up the single doses. While Beattie's partner went off to get the warrant, Jim watched the pusher finish his chore, tidy up the work table, and hide the bag of capsules in the chimney. Having seen the whole caper it was simple to make the arrest and seize the drugs before the culprit could do a thing about it.

By the mid 60s, newest members of the force walked the outside beats, senior constables walked the inside beats and, from beat #1 it was a short step to patrol car duty. From car work there was a choice: traffic or detective office (CID) of which the elite job was with homicide. This hierarchy resulted in very definite specializations while the beats began to signify punishment. Occasionally though, as with constables Kavanaugh and Lyall for example, patrol car officers asked to be assigned back on the street because they missed the interaction with the community.

During the late '60s and early '70s when the police and Mayor Sykes were at loggerheads, rock-concerts appeared on the social scene to further complicate the lives of our peace officers. The first big local rock festival was scheduled for July 4 and 5, 1970. Based upon reports of difficulties encountered with such gatherings elsewhere, a nine-part preparation program was undertaken by the police under Chief Kent.

A senior officer was sent to Toronto and Winnipeg to observe other centres' handling of rock-concert crowds; liaison was stepped up with RCMP drug experts; consultation was inaugurated with experienced Vancouver police; local immigration authorities were consulted; the availability and effectiveness of emergency medical services were determined; consultation was instituted with residents adjacent to anticipated rock-concert gatherings; the collaboration of young people was sought to aid policing procedures; an RCMP riot squad based at Sarcee Barracks was alerted; and all police on duty at the gathering were ordered to be unarmed and to not enforce the law except in extremely serious situations.

When the rock gathering was over, along with odd incidents of nudity, alcohol and drug misuse, and a few squabbles, The Calgary Herald declared the festival to have been a cheerful success and the police handling of it an excellent job. A quarrel between the mayor and the rock-concert promoter soured the situation and the two dissidents had to be separated by Deputy Chief Gilkes and the RCMP's Sergeant Collins. Apparently Mayor Sykes let the echoes of his displeasure with the peacemaker police linger, for it became a major factor in the mandate of a body of inquiry into the conduct of public business of the Municipality of Calgary.

The commission, headed by the Honourable Mr.Justice W.G.Morrow of Yellowknife, N.W.T. had as its other members Aldermen John Ayer and Roy Farran, who were members of the police commission. They felt the civic body had become political, with Farran saying the opening of its meetings to a larger public audience had turned them into a "Roman Circus."

Chief Kent testified that the police were being "thrown to the wolves." Deputy Chief Gilkes reported that the rock festival policing was conducted with the peace and safety of the entire community in mind. Sergeant Crosby-Jones, vice-president of the police association, reported the discomfort of the police at not being free to enforce liquor and drug laws at the festival.

For his stance before the commission, Chief Kent was lauded by the Calgary Police Association through their spokesman: **"Every member of the Calgary City Police under your command can now walk with renewed pride and dignity in the light of your testimony....Your bold stand on vital issues affecting the force and particularly the moral factor, has earned for you an enviable and lasting place in the affection and respect of the men and women of this force.**

"At a critical turning point in the history of this Department, your fine qualities of leadership were never more essential to our well-being, and have this day given us all a sense of purpose and direction. The old force will never be quite the same again, now that we have had an opportunity to take public issue with those

who seek to undermine the reputation and effectiveness of the Calgary City Police."

Mr.Justice Morrow recommended that the police commission cease holding disciplinary meetings in public and, following provincial government acceptance of his report, legislation was set in motion for the future composition of the police commission within the terms of the Police Act of Alberta. Resultantly, no longer would the majority of commission members be politicians, nor would a politician be chairman of the commission.

Chief Kent's time included some of the most difficult years the force had ever known. In addition to coping with an unsympathetic mayor and police commission, society was undergoing rapid and substantial changes. For example, mixed drinking and Sunday movies had become legal, and the rights of traditional authority were being challenged to a bolder degree which, for some people on the fringe of law-abiding society, spawned an increasing number of murders and violent and sophisticated crime.

In the early 1970s Superintendent Lyall was especially interested in vehicle theft and became quite a specialist. He developed a technique of restoring erased serial numbers with acid. One prosperous local businessman reported his Lincoln car had been stolen. Lyall's painstaking sleuthing revealed that the man, taking advantage of Alberta's loose car registration procedures, had used a fictitious number, waited, then had reported the non-existent vehicle stolen in order to successfully collect $7,000 insurance.

Lyall eventually uncovered a massive ring that stretched from Nicaragua to Alaska. Vehicle thefts included motorcycles, automobiles, motorhomes, boats, heavy machinery, and aircraft. Calgary was the main stolen-auto outlet that implicated mechanics, drivers, bodymen, and accountants, all part of a Dixie Mafia. Lyall's investigation, involving cooperative efforts of police in such major stolen-car sources as Dallas and Savannah, took him 4 years to crack and opened the eyes of the Calgary Police Department to the extent and intricacies of international crime.

A most impressive example of the Calgary force's innovative persistence occurred in the spring of 1971 following the murder of a local schoolteacher. Key evidence in the case was a man's cufflink which the suspect admitted having lost, not realizing the police had pried it from the dead woman's back. Detective Sergeant Ernie Reimer and Detective Ed Madsen secured an admission of guilt from the suspect but they still lacked conclusive evidence linking him with the actual slaying.

The victim had been bitten several times during the attack and Ernie Reimer remembered having heard of an English dentist's theory that a person's bite is as individual and distinctive as a fingerprint. With the suspect's permission Calgary dentist Gordon Swann made plaster molds of his bite. Dr. Swann then was sent to England for forensic orthodontal consultation and advice. Upon his return his evidence was accepted in court. Moreover, additional sleuthing linked the accused with three similar sexual assaults and murders in central Canada, for all of which he was convicted.

Although several years later United States police claimed to have been first in this field of detective work it was, in fact, the Calgary police who obtained North America's first "bite conviction."

As the 1970s progressed, the police found themselves becoming a major target in the rising tide of violence. Chief Kent and Gilkes, his deputy, were mentally and physically exhausted and announced they would be taking early retirement. This created a major problem of finding a leader capable of filling the chief's shoes. There was considerable disagreement as to who it should be, a local man or an outsider for, with Gilkes' departure, no name came readily to mind.

Out of the blue Calgarians learned the next chief would be head of the Oakland California Police Department, Charles Gain, who was considered to be the most suitable applicant. There was an immediate press, public, and police department uproar. Gain, sensing the hostility, and upon the advice of police association representatives who visited him in Oakland, resigned before ever taking office. The commission resumed its search for a chief, meanwhile appointing highly-respected George Kemp temporarily to head the force.

George W. Kemp agreed to delay his retirement and act as chief until a new man was found. He occupied the position from August 1972 until January 1973.
(Photo: Calgary Police Service Archives)

Kemp had no desire for the top job, making it clear that he would do his best on a temporary basis for he had his goal set on taking his pension in a few months. Meanwhile it was obvious the Calgary Police Commission was seeking an outsider. They found one in a young RCMP superintendent stationed in Victoria, B.C., Brian Sawyer. A quiet man who had spent much of his time with the mounties as an administrator Sawyer, even though he had not applied for the position, agreed to come to Calgary for an interview.

He impressed the commission, especially because of his firm and outspoken views on the positive role the police could and should play in the community. When the talks were over, the Montreal-born Sawyer expressed his hope that he would be offered the job he interpreted as a challenge that obviously fitted him like a glove. Soon afterward the commission made its choice and Brian Sawyer sent his acceptance.

The new chief had completed 21 years with the mounted police, serving in Nova Scotia, Ontario, Saskatchewan, Alberta, British Columbia, and the North West Territories. Starting as a constable he had achieved the rank of superintendent, meanwhile earning a

Bachelor of Commerce degree from Concordia University. Not since Toronto detective Alfred Cuddy had been named chief in 1912 had an outsider sat at the chief's desk. Moreover, Brian Sawyer was the first member of the RCMP ever to be taken on strength by the Calgary Police Department at a rank higher than that of constable.

Oddly, his chief ally probably was Charles Gain for, while Sawyer was not from within the community, somehow the public and the force did not view him as a "threatening foreigner" parachuted into the role. Brian Sawyer had a lot going for him. He was a career policeman with more than two decades as a working cop and as a police administrator with a profound awareness of the importance of personnel relationships.

The new chief came to the job in November 1972 but, until George Kemp retired early the following January, he was able to meet, listen to, and evaluate the men under his command, and to examine the scope of the job, while leaving the day-to-day details to Kemp. Right from the start he left no doubt that he

Sawyer, a long-time RCMP officer, took office as Chief of the Calgary Police Service in January of 1973. He stayed until August of 1984.
(Photo: Calgary Police Service Archives)

was the boss. Some staff members felt the new regime spelled incompatibility, so were encouraged to make room for others.

Chief Sawyer had inherited a very desirable aspect of police relations. It was the annual Police Expo that took on new significance when the police recruit training program was incorporated into the teaching curriculum of Mount Royal College. Students of nursing, geology, and aviation now came into contact with those learning police work and saw it as one more field of occupational study. The resulting recruiting program went a long way in establishing good police/community relations, especially among young people.

Immediately after Chief Sawyer took office he proclaimed new approaches in the fight against crime: "**...increasing emphasis is being placed on the prevention of crime as opposed to the apprehension of the criminal. The latter is seen as a defensive and reactive approach; the former requires an offensive and aggressive plan to combat crime problems before they occur. The concept to be developed by the Calgary Police Service will take into account the experience of several progressive police departments in Canada, the United Kingdom, and the United States, but will be designed primarily to fit Calgary's needs and expectations. A reorganization of the Department and significant changes in manpower deployment will undoubtedly flow from these studies. It is the development and implementation of this program that will be the major objective for the Calgary Police Service in 1973.**"

To be successful, changes had to openly involve personnel. So Chief Sawyer created a two-deputy setup with a strong team man and dedicated leader, Howard Leary as senior deputy chief. Sawyer knew he had much to learn about policing a large, dynamic city and Leary was a splendid teacher. Outspoken Inspector Alex Forster was appointed to the other deputy chief position.

Newly-promoted Inspector Ernie Reimer, Sergeant Paul Duros, and Constable Ken Handy were sent to eastern cities on a study trip. Western and southern municipal police operations were examined by newly-appointed Inspector Ed Madsen, Sergeant Kevin May, and Constable Harley Johnson. The assignment was to study, on site, the "nuts and bolts" approach to community policing.

Meanwhile, for the first time, all senior men and the rookies found themselves in conversation with the chief, exchanging ideas about doing a better job, getting close to the community. Upon their return, the roving teams shared what they had found and one result was a basic change in Calgary policing philosophy. Known as "zone policing" it is the realization that crime is a community concern and the police are only an extension of a community. For police to be effective each constable, in a broadened role, must be able to make decisions, with the result that many hitherto CID functions devolved upon the patrolling constables.

The final zone, of a total of 28, became operative in 1974. Calgary was divided into 4 districts, each under the command of an inspector. Each district within a particular zone was commanded by a zone sergeant. In effect each district inspector had to see to crime prevention and decision making in his territory wherein he was like the chief of a small force of about 100 men. This setup demanded responsibility and accountability that had a satisfying feeling of continuity. Instead of men being moved about town each month, under the zoning policy, constables' assignments were for about two years. Citizens benefitted from continuity in the handling of their complaints; constables got to know their community and their responsibilities within it; local trouble-makers were identified and pinpointed, and their problems handled with consistency.

Typical of the way this new regime worked was the case of Detective Sergeant Alex Penner in 1973. He was a CID man in charge of morality and liked investigative work. The chief asked him to become the inspector in charge of "B" district that included most of east Calgary, Forest Lawn, Inglewood, and downtown Calgary. It contained 6 zones and a resident population of 66,040 plus a lot of transients.

Penner was not at all sure he could handle that sort of administrative autonomy but, to his credit, decided it was a case of either grow or stagnate. Alex Penner not only made a rousing success of it, he became an enthusiastic booster by using another newfound skill, that of publicly explaining to people of the district the meaning and philosophy of the crime-prevention role within the community.

The police cars we know as the "blue and whites" were another Sawyer idea. The large word POLICE has a noticeable effect, because of its high visibility among speeding and careless drivers. Also it spreads a certain degree of reassurance among those whose conscience does not trigger a frantic desire to scuttle down a near-by alley! And Chief Sawyer shrewdly changed the name from "Calgary Police Force" to "Calgary Police Service" feeling it more accurately represented the police role in the community.

Calgary police cars took on a new and distinctive look in the early '70s, when they were painted in the now-familiar blue and white colors. This photograph shows the first unit to bear the new colors.
(Photo: Calgary Police Service Archives)

Another effective Sawyer innovation was the upgrading and refining of recruiting practice. Rather than hiring a lot of young fellows, then after a testing period weeding out those unsuitable for the job, qualifications were stiffened. Starting in 1974 all candidates were given a polygraph test based on questions covering their past. In 1975 candidates' psychological testing was made mandatory. No longer was walking an outside beat the somewhat patient lead-in to police work. Beginning back then, so it is today that the rookie is intensively trained from his date of acceptance and is expected to perform at a high level of professionalism right from the start.

No longer is it enough for sergeants and inspectors to be good police officers. They must have the professionalism of supervisors and administrators. To this end, in setting the trend, Chief Sawyer detailed all officers to middle-management courses and encouraged personnel to take post-secondary courses at Mount Royal College or at the University of Calgary.

Mount Royal College in Calgary saw many hopeful police science students pass through its halls. Seen here is Class #62 at work in 1975. *(Photo: Calgary Police Service Archives)*

Recruit Class #62 at Mount Royal College in 1975. The subject of discussion is Code 300s (Weapons Complaints). *(Photo: Calgary Police Service Archives)*

Training moves from the classroom to the track, where driving skills are sharpened. *(Photo: Calgary Police Service Archives)*

Investigation courses provide
students with the skill,
knowledge, and procedures
necessary to conduct
successful investigations.
*(Photo: Calgary Police Service
Archives)*

Weapons handling is a serious
business, and all serving
members undergo regular
testing on the range.
*(Photo: Calgary Police Service
Archives)*

The Calgary Police Service
tug-of-war team,
photographed at Heritage
Park in 1973.
*(Photo: Calgary Police Service
Archives)*

Samples of the success of this new direction are heartening and many. Early in his career, but after 9 years on the job, Constable Larsen was bitterly disappointed when he failed to make sergeant. Determined to prove his administrative and supervisory talents, he took a 5-year university course on his own time. After long stretches of foregoing some of the social pleasures, he graduated and the police promotions began coming his way.

Two members of the Calgary Police Service Canine Unit.
(Photo: Calgary Police Service Archives)

Harley Johnson was another successful student. He earned his B.A. at Calgary and his M.A. in public administration at Queen's University, Kingston, earning both degrees in just 3 years.

Sergeants Don Morse and Bob Hall behind the desk.
(Photo: Calgary Police Service Archives)

The year 1974 marked the addition to the service of other special studies, duties, and interests. The Arson Squad was formed and a highly successful and busy start was made on Neighborhood Watch. During its first 3 months of operation, it generated 698 calls. Then, as the 1970's progressed, a $4-million program of headquarters expansion and renovation was undertaken, the motor vehicle records system was computerized, a start was made on case file computerization, and a change in jail control resulted in the release of 20 policemen for other duties.

The civilian staff component of the
Calgary Police Service continues to grow.
(Photo: Calgary Police Service Archives)

The Tactical Team requires a
variety of skills from those
who are assigned to it.
*(Photo: Calgary Police Service
Archives)*

A member of the Bomb Dis-
posal Squad lowers a package
into a containment vessel.
*(Photo: Calgary Police Service
Archives)*

Constable Ron Wilson, a
member of the Support
Tactical Team, operating a
device called a 'remote
mechanical investigator.' The
machine is designed to be
useful in hostage situations and
for bomb disposal.
*(Photo: Calgary Police Service
Archives)*

Paper constitutes a significant percentage of police work, no matter what the operation.
(Photos: Calary Police Service Archives)

At about that time the district setup was restructured and a new downtown core "E" District came into being. The addition of it was indicative of the city's consolidated growth, as was the formation of a pair of Tactical Teams. These 6-man groups trained for a total of 2,000 hours before being assigned to duties that focussed upon weapon-related incidents. It is at this juncture that anyone who has experienced or, as a later arrival has closely observed, the growth of Calgary can see what astounding changes have been necessary in the growth, makeup, and development of our police service.

Gone for all time is the simplicity of learning the damage of a lawbreaker's caper, of seeking and finding him, and of ensuring he is brought to justice and fairly punished. With the condensation of a community's people and services, needs and acquisitions, misdemeanors and follies, so the inevitable complications of life in the human beehive place additional burdens upon the shoulders of our partners, the police.

A familiar link with the past for many Calgary citizens and police officers alike is this 1946 Chevrolet paddy wagon. In service for 23 years, it was finally auctioned off in 1969. In 1977 it was re-purchased for restoration and is now a regular feature at special events.
(Photo: Calgary Police Service Archives)

For example, within the new walls of the expanded police head-quarters was created a complete physical fitness area with its full-time fitness coordinator; a sophisticated shooting range; new crime-prevention programs that soon expanded to become part of the city-wide scene. One was "Operation Identification" in which policemen urged and instructed citizens in the permanent marking of household effects, hopefully to reduce an incentive to household thievery and to enhance the recovery of stolen goods.

A "Lock It Or Lose It" program was aimed at encouraging motorists not to leave keys in their parked vehicles. A new Community Services Section had the specific job of teaching 7,000 employees of stores, banks, and other financial houses "robbery prevention" procedures. As a decal on a dwelling indicating the contents had been marked sharply reduced household robberies, so the lectures on business hold-up procedures resulted in several arrests and an easing of the rash of robberies that had broken out all over town.

The Calgary Police Service Mounted Unit appeared 55 years after its predecessor had been disbanded. Remote areas of the city that had become favorites with increasing numbers of joggers and cyclists clearly needed patrolling following some unpleasant incidents. A mounted unit turned out to be an obviously ideal choice.

The Mounted Patrol Unit reappeared in Calgary in 1975 and since then has demonstrated that horses can still be effective in police work.
(Photo: Calgary Police Service Archives)

Another police activity that would never have been dreamed of as a necessity in simpler days was a Race Relations Unit. Then came a Family Consultant Unit that involved a police co-ordinator and 4 crisis workers based in "B" District. Efficient and swift response to calls for help became much enhanced by the introduction, in 1982, of the Computer Aided Dispatch (CAD). That instrument was yet another step in electronic cross-referencing that had become so vital a part of modern community peace-keeping.

Unfortunately, because people are what they are, the number and variety of crimes kept pace with society's increasing brutality. To an even more vital extent it fell upon the shoulders of the police service to maintain the partnership and to avoid being placed in an adversarial position within the community. The officers' greatest allies were electronic devices that, although unable to anticipate conflict, certainly speeded with increasing accuracy the apprehension of criminals.

The years 1980 and 1981 saw Calgary reach the apex of its newest oil boom, and as new people poured into the city, the crime rate flourished. There was a certain revival of the raw western frontier atmosphere, especially among newcomers who during the warm summer months appeared to be "trying the city on for size" by holding block-sized parties that almost invariably spilled onto the streets.

The police service consulted its fire-fighting compatriots in search of a solution to effectively quell the disturbances. One evening firemen, hastily summoned to an especially boisterous party, hosed down about 200 drunken revellers, effectively dampening their enthusiasm. The police thought this was just great and found, in a high-pressure sewage-cleaning truck, the ideal vehicle with which they could perform party "baptisms" on their own. It was never used even though one party of 500 riotous teenagers attacked a police cruiser. In an especially smart public relations move, the trashed vehicle was put on display on the Stephen Avenue Mall as a graphic example of the outcome of over-indulgence and mob irresponsibility.

Five hundred over-enthusiastic party-goers expressed their *joie-de-vivre* one evening by remodelling a police cruiser - while the officers were still inside. Workers in the downtown area evaluate the product of their fellow Calgarians' labours.
(Photo: Calgary Police Service Archives)

During the early 1980s the Oil Patch had a stranglehold on the job market, and the Calgary Police Service had some difficulty attracting suitable recruits. Superintendent MacNeil's staff development people, at one point, used a locally-inspired advertising idea:

**"JOIN THE CALGARY POLICE AND DRIVE
A COMPANY CAR"**

"You'll like our company cars. They're clean and flashy, with lots of interesting lights and a humdinger of a horn. They come with free gas, insurance, and a partner to talk to."

The ad raised a few eyebrows but it brought results that were sorely needed. For example, when the department put out a call for new men in 1981 it received 4,800 applicants but only 155 were suitable. The next time around most of the 425 recruits were new arrivals from eastern Canada lured here by the alleged glut of big-paying job opportunities.

Despite all the additional duties and functions, the local economic downturn of 1983 created a new manpower situation. For the first time since the Depression of the "Dirty Thirties," the police did no recruiting. On the contrary, 53 young constables were laid off, 24 of them from the same recruit class. Having received 16 weeks of basic training they graduated and were let go the same day. It was a bitter blow for them all, especially for those who had pulled up roots in central and eastern Canada purely in order to become Calgary police officers. These particular men and women were promised the inside track in future hirings, but the civic freezing order that blanketed all departments made prospects pretty bleak. Happily, by the end of 1985 most of those young graduate recruits were taken on strength.

One positive result of the job freeze was that those who had been preoccupied with recruit training were able to focus all their attention on refresher course instruction. They were able to catch up on those activities that, due to intensive recruiting, had been somewhat neglected.

The economic turndown had widespread effects, one of the more heartening being a dramatic reduction in crime. In no urban Canadian area was that drop as drastic as in Calgary. Some crime rates fell as much as 25% from 1981 levels and much of the credit was directed at Block Watch and Crime Stoppers campaigns. There was a healthy trend as people began to care a bit more for the welfare and safety of their neighbors, and all appeared to endorse a greater community awareness of the work of the police. In 1983 citizen awards were made to 64 Calgarians by the Calgary Police Commission, some of the recipients having risked their lives helping police apprehend criminals in their neighborhoods.

The crime reduction did not mean there was an absence of serious crimes locally, but it did seem to indicate that the police were at least winning some of the battles if not the war itself! Most certainly their "tools of the trade" were much sharper. The first experiment with an electronic aid was in 1969 with a microfilm scanner that instantly revealed the registered ownership of vehicles.

The City of Calgary, faced with its own need for swifter and more detailed information, formed its Data Processing Service. Access to this technology was afforded the police service and advice regarding police needs resulted in the acquisition of a computerized system for handling traffic tags which became operational in November 1974. Incidentally, the system was handling 400,000 tags annually by 1985.

Inspector Jaggard, with city employees John Macey and Theo Van der Putten, expanded and integrated electronic "assistants" into a Police Information Management System (PIMS) that had grown with use and in usefulness through modification and expansion. Items as diverse as the makeup of an offender and the workload of an officer are handled in seconds rather than in hours or days.

A Crime Information Centre evolved from a visit to Britain by Detective Ray Palardy who studied one overseas unit devoted entirely to keeping track of known, active criminals. It appears that 90% of crime is committed by 10% of the population. A card identification setup was replaced by a computerized investigative system inspired in part by a Canadian Police College course in Intelligence Analysis attended in Ottawa by three Calgary constables.

On parade during a 'Meet Your Police Day' event at Heritage Park in 1983.
(Photo: Calgary Police Service Archives)

Each forward step of this kind leads to another in the fast-paced and relentless electronic crime-fighting process. On one hand it is very

The Motorcycle Drill Team performed to crowds at McMahon Stadium in 1983.
(Photo: Calgary Police Service Archives)

expensive; on the other it adds tremendously to the time-saving effectiveness of the service. Its accuracy and thoroughness also gives the men and women in uniform a greater degree of protection and confidence than would ever have been believed possible.

Human changes occur too, of course. One of the newer ones was the surprise announcement by Chief Sawyer that he was resigning. When he took the job in 1972 he averred nobody should be chief for longer than five years. He modified that a bit as time went by, but on May 1, 1984 he announced he would leave the Calgary Police Service on the final day of August in order to become Alberta's provincial ombudsman.

Nine applications were received from would-be replacements. The police commission had declared the appointment would be an internal one and Deputy Chief Ernie Reimer was the obvious choice. A 30-year veteran of the service, Reimer became Calgary's 16th chief constable on September 1, 1984. He brought to the chief's job his experience as a street-wise patrolman, traffic officer, dog handler, homicide detective and, administratively speaking, deep involvement in zone policing and community commitment.

He was exactly what the police commission wanted as the next chief.

Chief Reimer swiftly did some reorganizing to achieve maximal efficiency within a restricted financial framework. He had no choice but to accomplish more with less, so starting at the top he reduced the three-deputy setup to one with two deputy chiefs. He consolidated police computer expertise within a new Information Management Branch directly responsible to Deputy Chief Madsen.

Ernie Reimer took over as chief in September 1984 and has held the position through the Calgary Police Service's Centennial Year. *(Photo: Calgary Police Service Archives)*

Next Chief Reimer created an Information Division to unite all areas of the service responsible for information and communication in the firm belief that efficient and reliable information is one of the vital keys to the success of the entire operation internally, and as a partner in the community.

A Communications Section dispatcher activates a remote transmitter receiver site. In 1985 Calgary Police Service Headquarters received a total of 614,463 telephone calls. Of these, 53, 598 were considered emergencies.
(Photo: Calgary Police Service Archives)

Two constables demonstrate a Mobile Data Terminal (MDT) to an interested citizen at a recent Meet Your Police Day.
(Photo: Calgary Police Service Archives)

Rapid access to information is one of the benefits of maintaining an electronic file system.
(Photo: Calgary Police Service Archives)

Vans which are utilized as mobile command posts during emergencies have proven themselves a valuable tool on numerous occasions.
(Photo: Calgary Police Service Archives)

Today complaints are handled at CAD (Computer Aided Dispatch) terminals, where trained personnel take calls and enter the pertinent information into the system.
(Photo: Calgary Police Service Archives)

Essential to increased efficiency was involvement with computers. It increased dramatically in 1985 with the addition of Computer Aided Dispatch and of an Automated Fingerprint Identification System. Old Chiefs Tom English and Alfred Cuddy would have wondered "What in hell did we start?" and shuffled off, shaking their grizzled, bewildered heads were they to hear today's constables glibly discussing their assignments in terms of the PIMS, ANGUS, PPAAS, CAD, and AFIS and all the rest of the beeping, blinking, clacketing electronic members of the service that, today, so efficiently inhabit police headquarters!

The pattern of reorganization was completed, one that still included an Executive Committee, a simple yet essential group in which each member had clear-cut responsibilities:

CHIEF ERNIE REIMER —
responsible for the Calgary Police
Service, the areas reporting directly
to him being: Operations Audit
Section; Finance Branch;
Psychological Services Branch;
Chaplaincy.

SUPERINTENDENT NORMAN
LUND — Executive Officer in the
office of the Chief of Police, and
responsible for: Internal Affairs
Section; Citizens' Complaint Unit.

DEPUTY CHIEF DOUG GREEN
— Chief of Operations. The Bureau
of Operations is responsible for:
Field Operations Division; Criminal
Investigation Division; Special
Crimes Section; Tactical Support
Section.

SUPERINTENDENT JIM LYALL
— Commander, Criminal
Investigation Division comprising:
Special Investigations Section;
Organized Crime Control Section;
Major Crimes Section.

SUPERINTENDENT DON
MACNEIL — Commander, Field
Operations Division consisting of:
Districts I,2,3,4, and 6; Traffic
Section; Community Services
Section.

DEPUTY CHIEF ED MADSEN —
Chief of Support Services. The
Bureau of Support Services
including: Information Division;
Headquarters Division; Planning
Section; Information Management
Branch.

SUPERINTENDENT
RON TARRANT — Commander,
Headquarters Division:
Headquarters Service Section;
Training Section; Personnel Section;
Career Development Section; Public
Affairs Branch; Media Consultant;
Duty Inspectors.

SUPERINTENDENT
JIM BEATTIE — Commander,
Information Division that includes:
Administration Section;
Identification Section;
Communications Section; Crime
Information Centre.

These eight specialist officers, each with a wealth of practical experience and mature knowledge, were in place to lead the service of 1985 into the second century of its guardianship of Calgary. On February 7th, the date a bylaw had been passed one hundred years earlier creating the force, a brief ceremony took place on the steps of City Hall. Chief Ernie Reimer presented a special commemorative sword to Mayor Ralph Klein. Sergeant Jarvis read letters of congratulation to the service from Her Majesty Queen Elizabeth II, the Prime Minister of Canada, Rt.Hon. Brian Mulroney, and the Premier of Alberta, Hon. Peter Lougheed.

On February 7, 1985, exactly 100 years from the signing of By-law No. 11 which created the office of Chief Constable and provided the duties of his office, Chief Ernie Reimer presented a commemorative sword marking the occasion to Calgary Mayor Ralph Klein on the steps of City Hall. *(Photo: Calgary Police Service Archives)*

The next evening, February 8, the Calgary Police Service hosted a Centennial Ball with 450 guests and 11 head-table dignitaries. It was a handsome affair with much ceremony, topped off by the official adoption of the proud emblem of the service, the Calgary Police Service flag designed by Sergeant Rod Jarvis. Dr.Ian Reid, Solicitor General of Alberta, on behalf of the government, presented the flag, official symbol of the service, to the chief constable.

A Centennial Committee headed by Superintendent Ron Tarrant coordinated the centennial year's events. Uniformed police men and women volunteers took part, for example, in the Boy Scout Annual Ice Stampede. The police presence took the form of displays, the pipe band, and the drill team, all assembled by Constable Bonnie Rothwell. A sword sub-committee under Superintendent Norman Lund produced a limited edition commemorative sword that depicts milestones in the history of the service on its blade.

The Calgary Police Service flag was officially adopted on February 8, 1985. Seen here with the new flag are (left to right): Chief Ernie Reimer (in historic uniform); Mayor Ralph Klein; and Brian Scott, Chairman of the Calgary Police Commission.
(Photo: Calgary Police Service Archives)

Members of the service staged displays at the HUDAC Home Show, organized a Police Half Marathon Race, and hosted the Northwest Police/Firefighter Olympics attended by 862 policemen and firefighters from the Pacific northwest part of this continent.

At the Calgary Exhibition and Stampede in July the Calgary Police Drill Team made its first official appearance, marching and playing in the parade in company with senior officers, the force's pipe band, the historic unit, and a contingent of retired members and civilian employees.

Over 100 police dogs and their masters from widespread points in North America were guests of the service in August during the National Police Dog Championship. The four-legged cops were put

Chief Reimer is congratulated by former City mayor and Alberta Lieutenant Governor, Grant MacEwan, at the Police Centennial Ball held February 8, 1985.
(Photo: Calgary Police Service Archives)

through their paces before a panel of seven judges that included two police dog specialists from West Germany. Another large group of police visitors converged upon Calgary to take part in the revolver competition known as the Canadian Police Combat Championship. More than 200 competitors were here, representing Canadian municipal police, the RCMP, and the U.S. Secret Service.

Memorabilia collectors were remembered too, as the service's centennial was marked by sales of special baseball caps, belt buckles, T-shirts, and lapel pins, along with 100 sets of badges produced with the help of the Glenbow Museum. These special remembrances were runaway best-sellers, their legacy being not only their personal memento value, but the sales made possible the purchase of drill team uniforms, a 1927 Harley-Davidson motorcycle for the police museum, and this centennial history book.

The Calgary Police Service flag, which was officially adopted February 8, 1985, is shown above being presented at a ceremony held at the opening of the new City Council chambers in December 1985. Chief Reimer made the presentation to Council.
(Photo: Calgary Police Service Archives)

As it completed its century of birthdays the Calgary Police Service ranked as the most modern, technically advanced, and philosophically progressive police force in Canada.

To endorse the intent of maintaining this enviable standing, Chief Reimer and the executive committee formulated a statement of the service's mission in these words:

TO OPTIMIZE PUBLIC SAFETY IN THE CITY OF CALGARY

The police service, in concert with other agencies and the citizens of Calgary, is instrumental in preserving the quality of life in our community by maintaining Calgary as a secure place in which to live. In so doing, we are dedicated philosophically and operationally to the concept of preventive policing. Our primary focus is on crime prevention, crime detection and apprehension, and traffic safety; and our most effective tools are positive community relations, education, and use of current technology to analyze conditions, project trends, and deploy resources.

LONG RANGE OBJECTIVES

1. To promote an understanding through the Service that the true measure of police effectiveness is the absence of crime and disorder, not the visible evidence of police action in dealing with them.

2. To secure the cooperation of the public in voluntary observance of laws by encouraging understanding and communication between the citizens of Calgary and their Police Service.

3. To maximize individual and collective skills within the Service in terms of crime prevention, crime detection, and traffic safety.

4. To promote a professional police image by demonstrating impartial service to the law, and by offering service and friendship to all members of the public without regard to race, religion, or social standing.

5. To use only the minimal force required on any particular occasion, and only when persuasion, advice, and warning are found to be insufficient to obtain public observance of the law.

6. To establish a recruiting, training, education and developmental capability within the Service that will maximize the potential of all members.

7. To achieve the foregoing within an acceptable cost framework.

Heading into the next one hundred years of policing Calgary, the immediate priorities set by Chief Reimer and his executive committee, in concert with the Calgary Police Commission, were as follows:

1. Develop programs to continue to enhance and revitalize Calgary's community-based preventive policing system (zone policing).

2. Define the magnitude and character of violent and sophisticated crime in Calgary and create related programs to counteract the growth of such crimes.

3. Develop and implement plans to contain costs of the Calgary Police Service and to increase the Service's productivity.

4. Create a Master Plan for the introduction of new computer-based communication and information

technology, including cost/benefit feasibility studies and implementation timetables.

5. Continue to create and nurture Human Resource Development programs, particularly those dealing with the issue of stagnant growth and a limited promotional opportunity environment.

6. Continue to coordinate and implement plans for security at the 1988 Winter Olympics that will complement Calgary's objective to present a superior world-class event.

Challenges continue to face the Calgary Police Service as the years pass, as members come and go, as one chief constable succeeds another. For each roster of uniformed men, women, and the officers who lead them, crime continues to be a community concern, and the police know they are only an extension of that community. A partnership, firmly founded and maintained between the citizens and the police, is vital.

Calgary is fortunate such an enduring bond of partnership has been forged. It has been achieved by the nurturing of patience, tolerance, understanding, and unwavering dedication of purpose.

The success of that team is a tribute to the men and women proudly wearing the uniform during deeply troubled and difficult times, as well as through the boisterous and triumphant ones, throughout the past 100 years.

IN MEMORIAM

Keeping crime at bay in Calgary has not been without price. During the first century of the city's police service, 7 officers have paid for their devotion and bravery with their lives. Remembering them, the living honour their fallen comrades, wearing behind the cap badge a black mourning patch. It is a constant reminder, and a tribute to those who died while on duty serving the community to which they had dedicated themselves.

CONSTABLE ARTHUR DUNCAN — July 2, 1917. He was a 12-year veteran of the Dumfries police in Scotland before emigrating to Canada. Duncan, at the age of 39, was shot and killed by a burglar whose loot he had uncovered during a night patrol at 8th Avenue and 8th Street S.W. His murderer was never brought to justice.

Constable A. 'Sandy' Duncan

Funeral of Constable A. Duncan, July 1917. Chief Cuddy (at left), members
of the RNWMP, and Calgary Police attended.
(Photo: Calgary Police Service Archives)

Funeral of Constable Duncan.
(Photo: Calgary Police Service Archives)

INSPECTOR JOE CARRUTHERS — June 13, 1933. The man nicknamed "Eagle Eye" by admiring comrades set up the Identification Bureau, and had an uncanny ability on the street to recognize wanted criminals at a glance. Carruthers was ambushed and killed by a prowler in the Scarboro area.

Inspector Joe Carruthers

CONSTABLE WILFRED JAMES COX — May 23, 1941. This popular officer was very successful at apprehending criminals. He was police force armorer, a magician at benefit concerts, and an expert marksman. En route to direct traffic at a funeral he was thrown from his motorcycle and killed.

Constable Wilfred Cox

Constable Ken Delmage

CONSTABLE KENNETH JOHN DELMAGE — November 6, 1957. Promoted to motorcycle patrol after two years on beat duty, Delmage was in collision with an automobile while en route to investigate a traffic accident. His death in hospital, as a result of injuries, resulted in the compulsory use, by motorcycle officers, of crash helmets.

Detective Boyd Davidson

DETECTIVE HUGH BOYD DAVIDSON — December 20, 1974. For outstanding police performance he was promoted through the ranks to detective in 1965. He helped set up the Arson Unit and was on the newly-created Drug Squad. He was shot and killed by a drug-crazed gunman who also lost his life in the shootout.
A Boyd Davidson Memorial Playground has been established in Calgary's Acadia district.

STAFF SERGEANT ALLAN KEITH HARRISON — March 12, 1976. With a history of beat policeman, traffic patrolman, and detective trainer behind him, Harrison responded to a hold-up alarm. While confronting the particularly vicious and drugged robbers of a credit union office, he was shot and killed.

Staff Sergeant Keith Harrison

CONSTABLE VASILI (WILLIAM) SHELEVER — May 26, 1977. Shelever joined the force in order to fulfill his dream of being of help to people. A month following his graduation he was questioning a gun-carrying suspect who shot and killed him at close range.

Constable Bill Shelever

**Those Who Cherish The Law In An Imperfect World
Remember And Respect The Gallantry
Of The Calgary Policemen Who
Paid The Ultimate Price.**

CALGARY POLICE SERVICE PERSONNEL
– 1985 –

The pages that follow contain photographs of
a cross section of Calgary Police Service
personnel who served in 1985. During the
centennial year there were 1181 sworn members
and 316 civilian personnel.

Calgary Police Commission

Office of the Chief

Bureau of Operations - Administration

Major Crimes Section

Special Investigations Section

Organized Crime Control Section

Special Crimes Section - Strike Force Unit

Special Crimes Section - Criminal Intelligence Unit, Interceptors

Special Crimes Section - Criminal Intelligence Unit, Support

Special Crimes Section - Criminal Intelligence Unit

Tactical Support Section - Mounted Patrol Unit, Tactical Unit, Canine Unit

Community Services Section - Administration and Office Staff

Community Services Section - Crime Prevention Unit

Community Services Section - Race Relations Unit

Community Services Section - School Resource Officers

Community Services Section - School Safety Unit

Community Services Section - Victim Crisis Unit

Traffic Section - Parking Control Unit

Traffic Section

Traffic Section

Traffic Section

1 District

1 District

1 District

1 District

1 District

1 District

1 District

1 District

2 District

2 District

2 District

2 District

2 District

3 District

3 District

3 District

3 District

3 District

3 District

3 District

3 District

3 District

3 District

4 District

4 District

4 District

4 District

4 District

4 District

4 District

6 District

6 District

6 District

6 District

6 District

6 District

6 District

6 District

Identification Section

Communications Section

Administration Section

Administration Section

Administration Section

Transportation Branch

Maintenance Branch

Training Section

Personnel Section and Career Development Section

Headquarters Service Section

Headquarters Service Section

Headquarters Service Section

Headquarters Service Section

Headquarters Service Section

Police Association

Chief Reimer (third from left) with members of the Historical Unit

Calgary Police Service Pipe Band